# INDIE AUTHOR CONFIDENTIAL 5

## SECRETS NO ONE WILL TELL YOU ABOUT WRITING

M.L. RONN

# ABOUT THIS SERIES

This isn't your typical writing self-help book. This series is a compilation of lessons learned from an indie author trying to walk the path to success. Follow author M.L. Ronn (Michael La Ronn) as he navigates what it means to master the craft of writing, marketing, and running a profitable publishing business. Learn from his successes and failures, and learn about things that most successful authors only talk about behind the scenes.

To read all the collected volumes of this series in an anthology, visit www.authorlevelup.com/confidential.

# CONTENTS

## BECOME A TECHNOLOGY AND DATA-DRIVEN WRITER

## BECOME THE WRITER OF THE FUTURE

## IDEAS YOU CAN STEAL

# INTRODUCTION

The second quarter of 2021 brought huge changes in my personal and writing life.

First, I completed my law degree. What a relief! Now I don't have to worry about reading gigantic books that take away from my writing time.

Second, I encountered a book called *The Conquest of Happiness* by Bertrand Russell. This book transformed the way I see my life. I made profound changes in my life in response to reading it. I'll share more later in the book, but the result was that I stopped producing "The Writer's Journey" and "Writing Tip of the Day" podcasts.

I've been stretching myself thin over the past few years, and I recognized that with law school behind me, it was time to start shrinking the responsibilities in my life. Working a full-time job, raising a family, running three podcasts and a YouTube channel, writing five to ten books per year, doing at least ten podcast interviews per year, speaking at five to ten engagements per year, and teaching six to ten insurance classes per year is just not sustainable. But, boy, was I doing it all and doing it at a crazy successful level.

So, I chose to leave many of those activities on a high note. In Q2 alone, I completed my final law class, taught my final insurance class, and released the final episodes of my podcasts. That's a seismic shift that I haven't been able to fully appreciate yet.

Bertrand Russell's book gave me a deep self-awareness about myself. While I was winding my activities down, I sensed that something new was coming—a new chapter in my life that I needed to prepare for. I didn't know what, but I listened to my spirit and spent a few weeks cleaning up my personal life.

Sure enough, shortly after all of this, a headhunter contacted me about a new job and made me an offer I couldn't refuse: an executive position at a global insurance company.

I wasn't looking for a job; it just happened, and the experience was surreal. In retrospect, this was the event my spirit was preparing me for.

I left a company for whom I had worked for 11 years, leaving behind friends and colleagues I knew well. I had a comfortable lifestyle and a good work-life balance that allowed me to build my writing career.

And it wasn't about the money, honestly. I knew that the new job was the right decision when, at the beginning of the fifth and final interview, the senior vice president of the company opened the interview with, "I noticed you like to write and read fantasy novels. Tell me your favorite series." When I told him that it was the Dresden Files, we spent the entire interview talking about Harry Dresden. We didn't discuss insurance at all. Not only did I land a rare executive position, but I also landed among colleagues who respected the writing side of my personality. That is incredibly rare in the corporate world.

I've said for years that my writing life and my work life feed off each other. I inserted a sentence about reading and writing in my LinkedIn profile—an act of courage in a very competitive world where showing an interest in the arts is often perceived as a professional weakness. That sentence helped me land a job. As an executive. At 33 years old.

If anyone needs proof that you shouldn't hide your creative interests from the rest of the world, let that be it. If your current employer uses it against you, find a new employer.

The new role came with enormous responsibilities. The first few months were intense. I worked 12-hour days, and I even worked on weekends to establish myself. Fortunately, the company I chose values work-life balance. I never receive emails over the weekend, and working long hours is always my choice, never mandated. Of course, because of my role, the work has to be done, and I know how to perform at a high level at work and in my writing.

The choice to scale back many activities made a tremendous difference in my ability to expand into this executive role without disrupting the other areas of my life too much.

That's precisely why I've spent the past decade investing in technology to help me be a part-time writer with full-time results. My preoccupation has been creating a writing business that runs itself. The new job put a big dent in my writing life for a few months, but now I'm (mostly) back to normal, writing the same way I used to.

During the time I was away, my Amazon Ads still ran. My books still sold on all retailers. I landed paid speaking engagements without having to lift a finger. I even generated an additional stream of income that will generate royalties for the rest of my life—again, without lifting a finger—licensing content that I created a few years ago. People still signed up for my email list, and my autoresponders fired like clockwork, selling books, and introducing my platform to new readers. My YouTube videos clocked record views and subscribers. That's how solid writing businesses operate in the 21st century—run by a founder who works a nine-to-five job.

And when I do need to be involved, I benefit from streamlined processes, advanced automation, and a team of assistants to help me accomplish tasks faster and more efficiently. I spend my time where it adds the most value—writing, marketing, and connecting with my audience.

Even though my personal life has changed drastically, my writing life has remained mostly the same.

I share this to show people what's possible if you work a day job. You can still build a writing business that you're proud of and be a world-class content creator.

Because of my job transition, this volume has slightly fewer topics than previous volumes, but you'll find it just as entertaining.

There are also three new changes:

- Moving forward, I'll be combining the Technology and Data sections. While both are important strategic priorities, they will not be a big focus for me in the last half of 2021 and 2022.
- This will be the last volume that contains Ideas You Can Steal. I will still capture ideas in this series, but I'll incorporate them into the other sections as I come up with them.

In 2022, I'll shift this series from quarterly to annually. I want to clear up more time to write fiction, so I'm reducing the scope of this series and the size of the volumes slightly to help me achieve that goal.

But for now (and always), you'll find a lot of interesting topics on these pages.

## My Core Strategic Priorities

As a refresher, my mission is to create content that entertains and/or educates my audience, preferably both, and to remain nimble in an ever-changing industry. I do this by focusing on five strategic priorities:

- Become a world-class content creator
- Become a world-class marketer
- Become a technology-driven writer
- Become a data-driven writer
- Become the writer of the future

I believe these five priorities are most important for me to have a long-term, sustainable career.

## What's in This Volume

In the World-Class Content Creation section, I discuss upgrading my YouTube studio and ending my podcast presence.

In the World-Class Marketer section, I discuss a lot of ideas related to cover design.

In the Technology and Data sections, I discuss my biggest achievement of the quarter: an automated editing engine. It's a victory on the level of my sales database in 2020.

In the Writer of the Future section, I muse on author job descriptions, thinking like an editor, and lessons learned from law school.

And, as always, I offer some fun ideas you can steal in your writing business. No volume of Indie Author Confidential would be complete without some bold ideas!

Enjoy.

*M.L. Ronn*
*Des Moines, Iowa*
*June 8, 2021*

# BECOME A WORLD-CLASS CONTENT CREATOR

# COMMA USAGE: A REFRESHER (FOR MYSELF)

While I was working on my automated editing engine last quarter, I discovered that I have a problem with commas. I understand their usage, and you'll rarely see comma splices in my work (actually, I hope you never see those). My problem is with consistency.

Take the word "too." Do you put a comma before it?

One of my editors believed I should. My current editor believes I should not. Is there a wrong answer? No, but I better be consistent in my usage so that every time I use the word "too" at the end of a sentence, I'm punctuating it consistently. This applies internally for every book I write, but also to my entire portfolio. This little rule is something that readers will never notice, but it's a quality issue that improves the overall presentation and consistency of my entire body of work.

That got me thinking about the "rules" of commas and how many of them can be addressed by automation.

Can I make my comma usage more consistent using automation instead of having to memorize rules? The less I have to memorize, the better.

I grabbed the following rules from the Purdue University Online Writing Lab (OWL) website, a well-respected website used my many schools as a reference for English rules.

## Rule: Use commas to separate independent clauses when they are joined by any of these seven coordinating conjunctions: and, but, for, or, nor, so, yet.

Example: I tried to stop crying, but I couldn't shake my emotions.

This rule is not programmable. My first question in researching automation and natural language processing (NLP) was simple: can computer software identify independent and dependent clauses?

In previous volumes of this series, I discussed NLP and how it can do part of speech (POS) tagging, which diagrams a sentence into nouns, verbs, adverbs, and so on. I assumed that it could also determine independent clauses.

I was wrong. Unfortunately, no open-source NLP programs that I know of can do this. That makes any grammar rule that relies on understanding the clause all but impossible. That said, programs like Grammarly and ProWritingAid can do this to some degree, but their methods are proprietary and not always accurate.

I spoke with a data scientist who specializes in NLP and he told me that English is a difficult language to perform NLP on because its grammar structure varies wildly.

Oh well. One day, when NLP can understand clauses, that will be a game-changer.

·  ·  ·

**Use commas after introductory a) clauses, b) phrases, or c) words that come before the main clause.**

Example: Because I was a student, I didn't have access to the company computer lab.

It might be better to phrase the sentence differently, like "I didn't have access to the company computer lab because I was a student," but the example is still a valid usage, and it explains why English can be so difficult.

This example also depends on determining the clause, so it can't be automated either.

**Use a pair of commas in the middle of a sentence to set off clauses, phrases, and words that are not essential to the meaning of the sentence. Use one comma before to indicate the beginning of the pause and one at the end to indicate the end of the pause.**

Example: I would love, if you have the time, to talk to you about my cousin Sarah.

Again, this rule can't be automated.

**Do not use commas to set off essential elements of the sentence, such as clauses beginning with that (relative clauses). That clauses after nouns are**

**always essential. That clauses following a verb expressing mental action are always essential.**

Example: It's important that, you go to the barbershop today.

That example uses the comma incorrectly. This rule is contemplated by most grammar checker apps today, and they should catch these types of errors.

**Use commas to separate three or more words, phrases, or clauses written in a series.**

Example: Lily, Ellen, and Dominique went to the store.

This rule is also already contemplated by most grammar checkers today.

**Use commas to separate two or more coordinate adjectives that describe the same noun. Be sure never to add an extra comma between the final adjective and the noun itself or to use commas with non-coordinate adjectives.**

Example: I bought a shiny, expensive car.

This is a tough rule because what constitutes a "coordinate" adjective is subjective. If I exchanged the word "shiny" with "red," then a comma wouldn't be required ("I bought a shiny red car.") If I exchanged the word "red" with "head-turning," then I would need a comma again ("I bought a shiny, head-turning car.") I'm not sure how you teach an AI to recognize nuances like these. Given that this rule applies to any noun and any series of adjectives, the combinations are limitless.

I've seen grammar checking apps attempt to police this rule, but not with any real accuracy.

**Use a comma near the end of a sentence to separate contrasted coordinate elements or to indicate a distinct pause or shift.**

Example: The door at the end of the hallway was red, like a beacon in the dark.

I can see some situations where this rule can either be grammatical or stylistic. In fiction, for example, an author may choose to use a comma for a dramatic pause. In a self-help book, though, you might easily be able to remove the comma without a reader even noticing.

**Use commas to set off phrases at the end of the sentence that refer back to the beginning or middle of the sentence. Such phrases are free modifiers that can be placed anywhere in the sentence without causing confusion.**

Example: Let's say that I rented a condo on the beach, shall we?

. . .

I don't believe this rule can be automated.

**Use commas to set off all geographical names, items in dates (except the month and day), addresses (except the street number and name), and titles in names.**

No examples are needed. This is perhaps the easiest comma rule that can be automated.

**Use a comma to shift between the main discourse and a quotation.**

Example: "Let's go to the store," he said.

This is also easily automated. Some grammar checkers already do this.

**Use commas wherever necessary to prevent possible confusion or misreading.**

This isn't something that can be automated, but it's an important guiding principle. When in doubt, ask if the reader will be confused. If the answer is yes, punctuate it so that they won't be.

There are other comma rules, but this was a fun thought exercise to show just how difficult commas are to tame with automation.

A decent amount of the suggested edits in my editing engine pilot came from commas, which makes this even more problematic.

I decided that the best way to address the problem (for now) was to refresh my understanding of comma usage, which is part of the reason I wrote this chapter.

# SEMI-COLONS

Earlier this year, I subscribed to the American Copyediting Society (ACES) as part of my automated editing engine project to help me better understand how editors see the world.

One week, they sent out a newsletter and included some book recommendations. One of those books was *Semi-Colon: The Past, Present, and Future of a Misunderstood Mark* by Cecilia Watson. It's a fantastic book that explores the history of the semi-colon, why it fell out of vogue, and why it deserves to still have a place in the English language.

Watson explores feuds between grammarians about semi-colon usage. She even discusses how a semi-colon sparked a massive court case in the United States.

The main takeaway from the book is that punctuation exists as a tool for authors to use. The field of grammar began as a way to standardize the writing of the English language because there were no punctuation (or even spelling) standards. Grammarians began with a lofty and noble goal of trying to make it easier for people to communicate with each other. However, the recommendations were often prescriptive.

Over the centuries, English rules have moved away from

prescriptive to suggested, and the *author* now makes the grammatical choices that are best for the work, not a grammarian. You could argue that it's always been this way, but it's hard to imagine a world where readers and critics expressed frustration at an author because of how they use semi-colons. Yet that was what happened to Mark Twain. In some respects, many authors in the past have fought hard battles so that we can use semi-colons as much or as little as we want today.

As for me, I like semi-colons; I believe that an author should use them whenever they feel it necessary.

# THE 5-5-50,000 CHALLENGE

I devised a new challenge to keep myself occupied while stuck at home. I called it the 5-5-50,000 challenge.

The idea: wake up at 5 AM for 5 days, write 5,000 words per day to arrive at a 50,000-word novel in one working week.

I wanted to do this project because I wanted to finish book two of my *Chicago Rat Shifter* series before my final law class began. I reasoned that if I woke up an extra 30 to 45 minutes earlier and focused on writing every day, looking for "cracks" to write in, that my word counts would add up in a big way. My goal was to dictate and write on my phone whenever possible.

It didn't happen.

I had some family issues that distracted me from the challenge. The first day, I hit around 3,600 words, which was respectable, but it was too far away from my ultimate goal. It was impossible to catch up, especially when I missed the goal on the second day.

But that's the nature of challenges. Sometimes you don't succeed. Perhaps one day I'll seek a rematch, but for now, it's on to the next challenge.

# WRITING IS MIND CONTROL

The best writing craft advice I ever received was "writing is mind control."

Readers see what you want them to see. You control the images that stream across their mind as they read your story. When you understand this, you can level up your writing because you can ask: "How can I control the story as the reader reads it?"

Through mere words that you type into a word processor in a certain order, you control what readers see, and to a certain extent, how they see it. You can even influence how they feel.

You can think of it as good or bad, but it simply is. Even an email or a blog post that you write has the same power. You can impart good or bad qualities to it, but it's neutral. The values you place on it are your own.

But it's important to understand that, as a writer, the words you use have power. Only when you understand that power can you learn how to wield it. As for you and me, we use our powers for good, and responsibly.

When you think about writing as mind control, you make

different decisions. Instead of focusing on typos, you instead focus on how to maximize your story's impact, how to intensify the images the reader sees, and how your message is being received. You don't get bogged down by technical details.

A lot of writers can't see past spelling and grammar errors, or plot. The moment you step away from those things (and can execute them competently), you have an infinite number of tools at your disposal to improve your writing. You start going deeper into the craft, and what you discover is weird, beautiful, and even crazy at times. That's the life of a writer.

Mega-bestselling authors exercise mind control. They know what you'll be thinking before you think it. As such, they give you exactly what you need when you need it to keep motivating you to turn the page.

What would it take to exercise this power in your writing?

I can't answer this question for you specifically, but I wrote a book called *The Writing Craft Playbook* that attempts to answer this question generally.

I explained this concept on my daily blog, and I used the words "writing is the act of getting inside people's heads and controlling their thoughts." One subscriber cautioned me and said that this line of reasoning scared them. They perceived it as me saying that writers should manipulate their readers.

That's not at all what I'm suggesting, though I acknowledge that this advice, in the wrong hands, could lead to that.

My logic is simple: I want as many readers as possible to keep turning the page and finish my books. I want to accomplish this as masterfully as possible.

How can I give readers what they want? What will make them bail from my story? Is there information I can give to help them see, feel, hear, taste, and smell the events in my story more vividly? I believe that asking these questions can lead to useful insights.

Ask those questions, and one day, you'll gain the power of mind control too.

# WHY I LOVE THE 3RD-PERSON POV

For my new urban fantasy series, *The Chicago Rat Shifter*, I swam against the current trend in the urban fantasy genre of using the first-person point of view. I enjoy writing in the first-person because of the intimate relationship between the viewpoint character and the reader, but it has significant drawbacks.

First, you can only describe what your main character is feeling and thinking. It's quite rare to see an urban fantasy series with multiple first-person points of view. The challenge with that is making each character's voice distinct, which is why I suspect most authors stay away from multiple POVs.

Second, your narrative is restricted to that one character. You can't jump into the heads of supporting characters or even villains. This makes the first-person point of view rather flat and limited from a storytelling perspective.

Authors who write in the third-person have more tools at their disposal to exercise the mind control that I referenced in the previous chapter. One of those tools is the ability to tell the story from the perspective of different characters. I missed that.

With *The Chicago Rat Shifter*, I wanted to tell an engaging story in the third-person so that I could explore different characters. Most of the chapters in the series are told from the perspective of my hero, Cyrus Grant. In the first novel, I split the remaining chapters between Cyrus's sister, Becca, and the villain of the story. Alternating between these characters allowed me to do a few things:

- I could switch the point of view to escalate tension and pacing;
- I could switch the point of view to give the reader information before the hero learns it, which is an underrated technique; and
- I could explore the background of the villain to make him more sympathetic, something that you don't often see in urban fantasy.

Did I succeed? I don't know, because I haven't published the series yet. But I was missing the third-person and wanted to hone my craft. When I committed to urban fantasy a few years ago, one of my fears was that I would forget how to do the third-person skillfully. As I think about future series, I will alternate between the first-person and third-person to keep building my skill in both storytelling styles.

# HEADER ILLUSTRATIONS IN MY NOVEL

I had an idea to take my book formatting to the next level: use header images for my chapters.

For my novel, *Dead Rat Walking*, I thought it would be cool to use images of rats intertwined with the chapter numbers. I've seen many traditional and self-publishers use header images in this manner. It adds flair and professionalism if done correctly. When done poorly, it looks tacky.

To accomplish this, I had to find an illustrator whose work matched my vision for the book. The illustrator would need to provide me with images for each chapter that I could load into Vellum, my book formatting software. Since the novel had 40-ish chapters, I needed at least 50 to 60 chapter illustrations based on the same pattern—one for each chapter number; I also had to account for the possibility that future novels in the series might have more chapters than the first novel. Once we settled on the illustration, it would have been a simple job to change the pattern for each number.

I shopped around for quotes, but I didn't find a freelancer that got me excited about their work. I started with Fiverr.com. I received hundreds of quotes, but most of the illustrators there specialize in children's books. Their designs were either too whimsical or not appropriate for an urban fantasy novel.

Next, I tried Upwork, and I found the freelancers there to be uninspiring for this project. It was probably bad timing.

Finally, I asked around for freelancers in my network who might be able to do this for me, but I didn't get any recommendations.

I decided not to proceed with chapter illustrations because I didn't want to settle for something that didn't match my vision.

I'm certain that one day in the future, I'm going to stumble across someone who will be able to do this for me, and I'll wonder why it was so difficult in the first place. But for now, I made my choice and moved on.

# PRODUCING HARDCOVERS

What would it take to produce hardcover editions of my books?

The idea has been on my mind for the last seven years, but I keep delaying taking action because I don't like the answers:

- I need to buy ISBNs. Due to the size of my catalog and my fast production speeds, I'll have to pay at least $1,600 for a block of 1,000 ISBNs. For something that doesn't generate a value-add, that kind of investment is against my religion.
- I need to redesign my book covers. Fortunately, around 2016, most of the cover designers I worked with automatically sized my book covers to be hardcover-ready, so this was smart thinking on their part.
- I need to redesign my interiors. Depending on the trim size I need, I may have to create a separate output from Vellum. That's easy, but it does require a few steps.

- I need to maintain two separate editions for my print books. From a data archiving perspective, that requires some thought, but it's not difficult.

If I'm honest, I just don't want to pay the $1,600 ...I can think of many things I can buy for that and get way more in return. For example:

- a new computer
- software upgrades
- new camera gear
- hiring an assistant for one-off tasks
- a course that will teach me a new skill that I can use to make money
- investing in more automation
- better bookkeeping services
- hiring a developer to create a better, more functional website to help me sell more books
- stocks, bonds, cryptocurrencies
- contributing to my retirement accounts
- keeping that money in savings for a rainy day
- hiring a marketing consultant to upgrade my branding
- hiring a designer to create a new logo for the Michael La Ronn and "Author Level Up" brands

I came up with that list in just a few minutes. After all, I'm running a business.

There are only four reasons to buy ISBNs:

1. To produce hardcover editions of my book. At the time of this writing, IngramSpark is the only place I would use to create a hardcover (but Amazon may

offer this in the future, which will be a game-changer).

2. So that my book sales will be tracked by data aggregation companies such as Nielsen, which helps reduce the "shadow industry" problem that self-published books have.

3. So that bookstores and libraries will take me seriously and stock my books on their shelves if readers ask.

4. So that, in the near future, I can bulk upload my books to retailers and make changes to my existing books without having to use retailer dashboards. StreetLib and PublishDrive both offer this feature, but you must have ISBNs to access it. The writer of the future will treat book uploads as a data concern, not a manual entry concern where you have to log in to multiple dashboards to publish a book.

Do I want hardcovers? Yes, they're a worthy investment long-term.

Do I care about contributing to the self-publishing data landscape? Sure, but not enough to break my piggy bank to do it. There are advantages to not having an ISBN—namely, industry-savvy people can't look up your book sales. But that's a topic for another *Indie Author Confidential*.

Do I care about bookstore or library sales? Not really. I'm not sure they'd want to stock my books anyway due to the bias against self-publishers, though that seems to be changing. If I become famous and readers want my books, then bookstores will stock them anyway.

Do I care about automated uploading? Absolutely. I've discussed this at length in previous volumes of this series. But I'm well ahead of my time and I only know of one other indie author who even dared to mention this on her blog (and almost no one cared). Authors aren't thinking about this yet, and they won't until enough big-name six-figure authors start demanding it. Then everyone will want it. But we're still a few years away from that, so I can bide my time.

So, I decided to put this on hold again. The worst part is that the longer I wait, the more painful it will be when I do make the migration to official ISBNs (not the free ones that retailers give). I'll deal with that when the time comes.

# A NEW WAY OF TEACHING

I bought a Wacom Tablet. I've always wanted one because I believe it's an instructor's dream.

There have been many times when I have wanted to draw something for my audience to help them understand a concept better. Writing is such an abstract field; if someone tells you that you need to "hook" readers, how the hell do you show that? We talk about showing and not telling all the time, don't we? So why don't we take that same approach when giving writing advice?

A question that I've always tried to answer is "how can I visualize the craft of writing?" I believe that if you can visualize the craft, you can teach it better. This is why my free book, *The Writing Craft Playbook,* has been a successful lead magnet for growing my email list. The book is a series of pictures that show how mega bestsellers hook readers. The pictures, which show illustrations of prose on a page with circles and X's, look like football playbooks.

I am surprised at how successful *The Writing Craft Playbook* has been. Ever since, I have wanted to level up the concept.

I downloaded a program called Open Board, which is open-source whiteboarding software that teachers use. And wow—it's fantastic.

Combined with screen capture software, I can use Open Board to create Khan Academy-style videos that let me draw on the screen, bring in videos, links, images, and many other things. I can draw wireframes, mind maps, playbooks, and so much more. I can even do this on livestreams. To my knowledge, this is unexplored territory.

In short, I like Open Board a lot. I also like the Wacom Tablet. I landed a speaking engagement with *Writer's Digest,* where I will be discussing the concepts in *The Writing Craft Playbook.* I'm using that event as a test run for the "look and feel" that I want to achieve with this teaching style. I will report on how that goes, but if it works, I will have created a new style of writing craft instruction for writers, one that hopefully helps break down abstract concepts in new ways to improve their writing craft.

# ENDING TWO PILLARS OF MY WRITING PLATFORM

This quarter, I decided to end two pillars of my platform that have been transformational for me.

The first was my podcast, "The Writer's Journey," which I started in 2018 to document my writing process and the behind-the-scenes musings of a part-time writer. At first, the show existed to give my true fans more content to serve them better. The show started in a highly scripted format, where I shared aspects behind the scenes of my books. I enjoyed the scripted format, but it was difficult to maintain.

I never thought that anyone would listen to the show, but it was surprisingly successful. After the first six months, I noticed that my book sales and my email subscriptions increased.

Over time, I expanded the show into an improvisational format. Instead of scripting episodes, I turned on the microphone and talked about what was on my mind. I opined on current events in the publishing industry, interesting thoughts I had about becoming the writer of the future, and other random thoughts that my audience found engaging.

I received emails from listeners all over the world: Europe,

Australia, New Zealand, the United States, Canada, China, Japan, and more. It made me smile to learn how people listen to my show; one listener tuned in during her lunch breaks; another listened while walking her dog; another listened while taking long walks on the beach. All my listeners had one thing in common: they liked listening to what I had to say every week and they never knew what they were going to get.

As I reflect on the show, the most popular episodes were those where I became vulnerable and shared things I was struggling with, like my decision to seek therapy for the abandonment issues I suffered from my biological father. I openly shared my experiences with therapy, and many people wrote to me privately to express gratitude because it helped them. I didn't expect that.

I didn't realize it at the time, but "The Writer's Journey" was talk therapy for me. Even though I wasn't talking about personal issues every week, the act of talking about my problems was therapeutic. I held myself accountable to talk about my successes, failures, and everything in between.

I mentioned earlier in this volume that I encountered Bertrand Russell's amazing book, *The Conquest of Happiness*. After reading that book, which is a treatise on how to be happy in your life no matter what your circumstances, I discovered that I didn't need to record "The Writer's Journey" anymore.

Podcasting was my way of dealing with inward issues. I talked them out. Russell's book served as a mentor, and it showed me just how effective podcasting had been in my life up until that point. It also taught me that I no longer needed to do it because I had healed the part of myself that made me feel that I needed to do it.

*The Conquest of Happiness* also played another part. Russell was a British aristocrat who was a suicidal youth, but he learned to enjoy his life through focusing externally on others and special interests and diminishing preoccupation with himself. That's one of the big pieces of advice in the book: diminish preoccupation with yourself.

Writers are, by definition, preoccupied with themselves. They have to be. I believe that writing, at its root cause, comes from pain. We just can't see that because the writing makes us feel good.

Am I saying that writers are conceited? No.

But we have to learn to diminish that preoccupation. I am no exception to this rule. The *Indie Author Confidential* series is about my writing life. It's 100 percent my opinions and anecdotes from my life. The crazy thing is that people enjoy reading about it.

On the one hand, I internalized Russell's advice and it felt natural to me, but on the other hand, here I was with a massive platform that is all about me. I felt that I needed to reconcile the inconsistencies.

The podcast served its purpose, and when I saw it for what it was, it was merely a preoccupation with myself. It just happened to be content that my audience enjoyed because I shared advice and talked openly about the behind the scenes life of a writer. Again, it was a very odd feeling to see an action you've been taking for so long in a different light, especially, when you built an audience around it.

I realized that if I wanted to continue doing what I wanted to do, which is help, entertain, and educate people through the written word, I couldn't keep doing it by producing a show that was only about me. I needed to focus my efforts on others. Russell helped me see that it was time for me to evolve and move onto the next level of service.

That's why I ended "The Writer's Journey." I didn't like

ending a show that had built up so many weekly listeners, but once I had this revelation, I woke up one morning with no topics to discuss for the show, which had *never* happened before. It was time to end it, even though it meant that my sales would diminish. And they did.

The second part of my platform that I ended was my "Writing Tip of the Day" podcast. I started it in 2019 as an early adoption of Amazon Echo flash briefings, but I also syndicated it as a regular podcast. Every Monday through Friday, I offered a short writing tip. The show eclipsed "The Writer's Journey" in 2020 and was, after YouTube, my second biggest audience.

Whereas my reasons for ending "The Writer's Journey" were personal, I ended "Writing Tip of the Day" because I wanted to end the show on a high note, and I was starting to run out of ideas for episodes.

I batched the episodes, recording months in advance. That worked well, but looking at the future, I had to either change the format of the show or end it. I wasn't prepared to change the format—part of the show's charm was that it offered exactly what listeners wanted—a crisp writing tip.

I don't believe in creating subpar content that I'm not passionate about. That's not good for listeners or my brand. So I ended the show.

These decisions are never easy. Many listeners had grown accustomed to listening to "Writing Tip of the Day" during their morning routine. I had looked forward to having the show be there for them as they emerged from COVID-19 lockdown and started going to work again. But hey, you've got to be true to yourself, and sometimes that means ending things that bring people joy.

However, I'm sensitive to the fact that no one likes to have their favorite show canceled, so I tried to account for this in a few ways:

- I ended the show on a high note, without sacrificing the quality of content leading up to the final episode;
- I explained to my audience why I was ending the show;
- I explained where my listeners can continue engaging with me, even though I'm no longer podcasting;
- I left up the backlist episodes for future listeners to discover, and I'll pull them down once people stop listening for good;
- I ended the show with a final episode that serves as an "end cap," telling people that I'm still alive and where they can find me.

It's not perfect, but I did the best I could. I hope people understood and respected the decision.

As a content creator, I don't want the "golden handcuff" dilemma. I don't want to be tied to the content I create to the point where walking away means ending my career or completely choking off my income. I've seen too many writers and YouTubers fall into that trap, and it's ugly. There are no good solutions. I've always said that I'll make content that I'm passionate about, and the moment I stop being passionate about it, I'll stop creating it.

At the same time, I don't want to come across as fickle. I don't want people to think "I don't want to follow Michael La Ronn because every time he starts something, it ends." For this reason, I typically commit to any initiative for at least two years. I don't start anything unless I'm prepared to continue it for at least two years. In today's digital landscape, two years is an eternity. 2020 was drastically different from 2018 , and 2018 was drastically different from 2016. What matters is staying relevant and true to yourself, and just like society, I too am a work-in-progress.

# NEW YOUTUBE STUDIO

Now that I've finished law school and ended my podcast footprint, I decided it was time to spend more time on my YouTube presence. I've been wanting to grow my YouTube channel but haven't been able to dedicate resources to it.

I recommitted to the future of my channel by rebranding it, doing data analysis into future videos that would bring new subscribers, and upgrading my equipment.

After upgrading my camera, lens, and lights, I rearranged my studio and created a new style for the channel.

As a person of color, I have always been sensitive about my camera appearance. I just couldn't seem to get it right. I started with a white background that mimicked classic Apple commercials, but the light was too bright and my skin was overexposed. Next, I experimented with shooting in my home office, but it was too dark, and the LED lights I bought were too harsh. Then, in my new house, I designed a set and bought equipment that was gentler on my skin, but it still wasn't good enough.

Now, finally, after seven years, I have a shooting style that is natural and flattering for my skin tone.

Here is the equipment that I bought:

- Canon M50 Mark II
- Sigma 16mm lens
- Elgato Key Light
- A camera reflector panel to fill in light on the side of my face
- Neewer LED Bi-Dimmable Lights (as background lights and a hair light)

If you're interested, you can check out affiliate links to my equipment by visiting www.authorlevelup.com/gear.

I have a small space, so I need an economical setup. The wide-angle lens lets me position the camera approximately one to two feet from my face without being an extreme close-up. And I still get a blurry background. The lens also does well in low-light, which means I can turn off all the lights in my basement and rely solely on my studio lights, something I couldn't do in the past.

Visit my channel if you'd like to check out recent videos with the new style.

# THE WONDERS OF LIVESTREAMING

I started livestreaming on my YouTube channel in 2020. Once a month, I hosted a "Writing Power Hour," a 90-minute stream where I invited my community to join and write toward their work-in-progress with me live. We wrote in 20-minute increments, with 5-minute breaks where I answered questions and had a lively conversation.

My power hours were a huge hit. This surprised me because I didn't think anyone would be interested.

In the last chapter, I discussed my YouTube studio upgrade. I also upgraded my livestreaming capabilities. Originally, I used StreamYard, which was free and easy to use.

For software, I upgraded to eCamm Live, which is dedicated streaming software for the Mac OS. eCamm has an amazing feature where it lets you use your DSLR or mirrorless camera as a webcam on Zoom, Microsoft Teams, Skype calls, and more. In other words, I can achieve the same look on livestreams as I can on my YouTube videos, which is attractive to me because:

- it instantly improves the quality of my livestreams

- it creates consistency with my regular, non-
streamed YouTube videos
- it improves my camera quality in future video
interviews
- it increases my professionalism for online speaking
engagements to a level that *no one* in the self-
publishing space is executing on, which makes me
stand out, leading to more speaking event invitations
in the future

This is why I invest in technology and future capabilities. Incremental improvements over time lead to massive advantages in the future. I'm already executing at an above-average level; the next levels promise even more amazing capabilities, and I'm the only one experimenting with this style right now. That's cool.

Admittedly, I was fashionably late to the livestreaming game. Many YouTubers have been doing it for years. But I'm doing it in my way.

# MAKING EYE CONTACT ON
## CONFERENCE CALLS

My new YouTube setup forced me to deal with a problem that I've always wondered about but never quite solved. It seems that I'm one of three people in the world who care about it.

The problem? Making eye contact on conference calls.

If I look at the person on the screen, my eyes are looking down. If I look at the camera, I can't see the person! It drives me crazy because I believe that even if you're on a conference call with someone, eye contact is still important. With my ALLi work as an Outreach Manager, I consider the ability to make eye contact especially important as I build relationships with key people in the publishing industry. Plus, being able to see someone properly means you can read their body language and respond accordingly.

Yet I am alone in my beliefs (again). In an era of working from home and "Zoom fatigue," people prefer to not even turn on their cameras.

However, I was working from home before working from home was a thing. The same problems with people turning on cameras then also exist now.

Here are a few reasons I think people don't like to turn their cameras on, and some of them are valid:

- People's homes are a mess.
- Their kids may be in the background.
- They may not feel comfortable putting their background on camera.
- They may be self-conscious about how they look on camera. (I once wore a shirt that did not play well on camera at all, so I turned my camera off for fear of making others sick.)
- They may be self-conscious about the lighting in their room. (I worked with a guy whose face was covered in shadows, making him look like a supervillain...on a work conference call.)
- They're not camera-ready; they might be wearing pajamas, or they haven't taken a shower yet.
- They keep the camera off to preserve Internet bandwidth.
- They're multitasking and don't want people to know. Hell, they might even be driving or shopping at the grocery store.
- They secretly don't like the person or people they're meeting with; they reserve camera time for people they like.
- They prefer to keep their cameras off to avoid accountability. It's a sign of disrespect, and the equivalent of hiding.

These reasons explain the reticence to turn on cameras when people are working from home.

However, if you put many of those reticent people in a different environment, with friends and people they like, talking about topics they're interested in—I guarantee they'll turn on their cameras.

In my writing and personal life, I make Internet calls all the time. Sometimes the calls are business-related; other times they're purely for pleasure and social interaction. No one has ever had their camera off. Not a single person.

But, I digress.

I just want to see people on conference calls and have them see me, and emulate in-person contact as much as possible. If you can look someone in the eye, then you're winning, in my opinion.

I researched solutions to this problem for weeks and found nothing that worked for my situation.

A few of the issues I faced:

- I have a small office space.
- My webcam sits on top of my computer screen, which means I have to look up to "look the camera in the eye."
- I need a simple solution because my job and writing life are fast-paced.
- I need a solution that works the same for work conference calls and podcast interviews.

I found a few videos online that recommended using a teleprompter to solve the problem. You position your webcam behind the teleprompter glass and use an iPad or camera monitor to reflect your conference call app onto the teleprompter. This way, you look directly into the camera, but the other person can't tell you're using a teleprompter.

I happened to have a teleprompter that I bought a few years ago, and this technique worked well, but teleprompters are bulky and complicated. It made my small desk feel even smaller.

I also found solutions where people used special devices that clipped onto your computer screen that served the same purpose as a teleprompter, but I didn't like those because they take up usable monitor space.

So I found my solution:

I bought a seven-inch camera monitor. Photographers usually attach these to the tops of cameras so the person being filmed can see what the camera sees.

- I bought a desk light stand. It clamps on my desk. Most people use these to hold ring lights. Because the stand has a threaded camera attachment, I attached the camera monitor to it instead and positioned it directly behind my webcam so that if I look into the camera, I'm also looking at the center of the camera monitor, which is directly at the person I'm talking to.
- I mirror my computer screen to the monitor that contains the conference call app.
- I bought a bi-directional HDMI switch so that I can switch the monitor between my work computer and writing computer with the push of a button.

That solved the problem completely. I feel so much better about my conference calls now, and they feel more natural.

I recorded a video on my personal YouTube channel about the setup if you are interested at www.authorlevelup.com/eyecontact. The video racked up 375 views in three weeks despite having a good thumbnail and strong production value. People just aren't interested yet.

But one day, when more people decide to solve this issue, my video will be there.

# BECOME A WORLD-CLASS MARKETER

# FOLLOW-UP THOUGHTS ON BOOK COVER DESIGN

In the last volume, I discussed my concerns around the future of book cover design. In short, I believe that we may be on the cusp of a designer shortage—existing good designers continue to raise their rates (and waiting periods) without providing higher quality in return (because their designs are good), and newer, less experienced designers don't provide a high-enough quality product. The gap between the two is where many authors will find themselves stuck—not able to afford higher quality designers but not satisfied with the entry-level designers. My conclusion was that, unless something changes, the best long-term solution for prolific authors like myself is to design their covers.

I made that conclusion reluctantly. I'm not thrilled about having to learn cover design, but I'm willing to do it to maintain my desired publishing speed if my predictions come true.

I received a wonderful email from a listener of "The Writer's Journey" who offered some advice on how to get started with designing your own covers. He's a designer by trade and has a lot of experience. I wanted to pass his advice along.

First, the companies that provide design software offer the

best tutorials, even though the material is dry. He recommended always starting there, especially with Adobe Photoshop and Affinity Designer, which are the two competing apps for most design tasks. Both programs have similar capabilities, but he preferred to work with Adobe for text. In fact, he frequently switches between the two apps because Affinity does other things better.

He recommended always working at print resolution. This means at least 300-350 dots per inch (300 DPI). Fortunately, this is just a setting you can apply once and not have to worry about it.

In his opinion, a curriculum for learning how to design your covers would contain the following "lessons" (learning them at an advanced level):

- Layers
- Layer blending (allows you to adjust the transparency of shapes and create textural and lighting effects)
- Layer-based color correction (helpful for combining multiple photos)
- Selection tools
- Eraser tool
- Eyedropper tool (to transfer colors consistently)
- Color washes (helps bring different photos into a unified color palette)
- Brush-based color correction
- Gradations (for emphasizing one area of your cover over another)
- Text settings; primarily kerning (adjusting the space between letters), ligatures and special characters, color adjustments, effects (drop shadows, embossing, bevels, and so on)

- Exporting a cover design for both ebook and print

What a lesson plan! Master these aspects of your design software, and you'll have the skillset to create a cover, even though you won't have designed one yet.

Once you learn these things, you can ascend to the next level of learning.

I thought I'd pass the advice along as I receive emails frequently from people wanting to do their covers but who have no idea where or how to start.

# THOUGHTS ON PERSONAL BRANDING

This chapter is long and meandering, but there is a lesson at the end.

I was invited by Matty Dalrymple to do a guest segment on her podcast "The Indy Author." My message was that branding is everything you do.

I recorded a 2-minute video on personal branding and how authors can improve theirs.

I specialize in personal branding. It's one of my superpowers. Sure, I'm not a good *designer*, so at first glance, my claims might appear to be arrogant and outsized, but consider my qualifications.

In my professional career, I've progressed through corporate America at a rapid rate for someone my age, and I've done it unusually.

First, personal branding is everything you do. The cliché "every day is an interview" is true in the digital age. Every time a reader comes into contact with your brand, you're interviewing for their attention. The same techniques that apply in the working world apply to writing. I'll explain why that's the case and how you can mine your personal experiences to improve your author branding.

How do you find a new job in today's digital age? In the past, it used to be that you had to know someone. That's why people put so much emphasis on "networking."

Today, while networking is still as effective as it always has been, there's a new way to find jobs: playing to search engine algorithms and automation. Many people still don't understand that no one looks at resumes anymore; computers do. A system scans your resume for certain indicators on whether you are a match for the job in question. If your resume matches those indicators, you'll advance to a screening interview. Even if you meet all the qualifications of a job, you'll be declined if your resume doesn't play nicely with the company's software. This means that you must use keywords from the job description and industry lingo on your resume to have a *long shot* at advancing to a screening. Read that last sentence again. Assuming you can get to a screening, then it all depends on your interviewing skills.

I am a *very* good interviewer. Even before I started podcasting and YouTube, I was highly skilled at verbal communication. My original major in college was Speech & Rhetoric (before they killed it—Rest In Peace). I've interviewed and gotten jobs that there was no way in hell I should have gotten. I got them because I knew how to work the system and I have a positive personality.

What do I mean by working the system, do you ask? I don't mean lying. And I certainly don't mean exaggerating my qualifications or experience. I never did that. I landed jobs well above my experience level with a slightly better-than-average work product.

The secrets? I'll list them and then explain.

- Be better than average.
- Learn how to "read" leaders in your organization and predict their future behavior at least three steps ahead.
- Choose your boss, and choose wisely; if your boss is chosen for you and that boss is bad for you, wait it out or find a new job. Refer to step #2. Never stay in a miserable work environment longer than necessary.
- As soon as possible, discern the "professional lessons" each job can teach you, and strive to learn them. These lessons are not what you think they are.
- Focus on my professional development.
- Do no harm.

**Be better than average.** Most people take the path of least resistance at work (and in life). Yet very few jobs are difficult. The jobs themselves are the easy part.

You can win big in life if you learn to execute on the same level as your peers, but then do little things that they would never think of (or want to do). This takes you from average to above-average.

(Note: In the professional world, you don't want to be the best. The best workers always have targets on their backs, and many would love to see them fail. You want to be good enough to catch the attention of the leaders in your organization while still commanding the respect of your peers. I know, I know—human nature. Please ignore this paragraph when it comes to your writing life.)

When I was a claims adjuster, customers complained that adjusters never called them back. Customers often had to wait days, sometimes weeks, to hear from an adjuster so they could get their cars fixed. I noticed that the longer a customer's voice-mail went unanswered, the madder the customer got. (Wouldn't YOU be angry if you went weeks without a car?) That led to *more* phone calls, escalations, and manager involvement.

Yet the prevailing opinion on the work floor was "I have too much crap to do. This angry customer can wait like everyone else."

I made it a personal goal to return voicemails within 24 hours, even if I had to sacrifice performance in other areas of my job. When other adjusters were trying to rush customers off the phone because of heavy workloads, I spent *more* time on the phone with customers. If they asked me about their policy, I'd send them a PDF and go through the coverages with them. Since I spoke Spanish, I worked with many Latino customers who didn't speak English. I offered to translate for them when they went to retrieve their cars from the impound, or when they went to the rental car company and needed an interpreter. My leaders always told me that I had a good "phone side" manner— I connected with people in ways that my peers did not, mainly because of my voice and my calm demeanor.

My customers were much happier than my colleagues' because I returned their calls. It's easier to settle a claim with someone happy with you versus someone angry at you for not calling them back. I settled claims so quickly, people thought I was cheating.

My manager received fewer complaints, which astounded him. He made me his "fixer"—he would send me the angriest customers and I would make them go away.

Guess who got the best customer compliments?

Not me. In fact, I seldom received thanks. I used to keep an "accolade" folder whenever a customer sent a thank-you note. In my five years as a claims adjuster, I received fewer than 20. Once customers got their cars fixed, they forgot about me and never answered the customer surveys. Many of my colleagues took that as a personal insult; I considered it an indicator that I did my job correctly.

My colleagues chased praise from customers. Some even begged customers to send their manager kind words, or to answer a "10" on the customer surveys. While they were doing that, I just returned people's calls.

At the end of the year, who do you think got a promotion and a pay raise? Me, all because I reverse-engineered the system. I then *built my resume* around those successes, which I could point out in my next job interview.

This method worked like magic. Interviewers would ask me basic questions, and I would come back with answers that shocked them and showed that I thought about things differently. Combine that with good performance results and a glowing manager recommendation, and boom—new job.

I kept building on my successes, and after a few years, I had a resume and a background that looked like no one else's, even though I had a similar work experience.

I consider my work experience to be a portfolio of assets, just like my books. When I net a professional victory, I find a way to package it so I can "sell" it in a future interview.

Before you start thinking that I'm vain, the best experience to sell is one that also develops you professionally because you can speak to how it developed you.

Here's how you sell an experience:

- Identify the pain point (it must be something that YOU uncover, not someone else).
- Tell what you thought about it (and don't mince words).
- Explain how you solved it, who you worked with (job titles), and the result in quantitative terms.

- Explain what you learned and why it's relevant to the job you're interviewing for.

**Learn how to "read" leaders in your organization and predict their future behavior.**

At one company I worked for, I noticed that news predictably flowed from the top-down.

- Low-level executives often received advance notice of a change at least one year to 18 months in advance. It was then their job to set a strategy within the directive to achieve it.
- Directors received the news around six months before the change. It was their job to operationalize the change, and because they knew the news but couldn't share, they would often "nudge" managers in a certain direction without telling them why.
- Managers received the news around one to three months before the change. By this point, the plan was already finalized and it was their job to deliver the (usually bad) news.

As a low-level employee, I used this knowledge to predict what was coming. Whenever workers received a "survey" about something or were asked to track their time for certain tasks, I could reliably predict when a change would be announced.

Once I knew the "when," I could read between the lines and figure out the "what" and then the "how." If the answers resulted in my job getting harder, I changed my behavior to align with what I thought was coming.

When reorganizations were announced, I studied the organization charts carefully. I observed that in a major company reorganization, there are always one or two "threads" left dangling; in other words, the moves didn't make sense, and if you pulled the threads, you could spot what the next reorganization would be.

For example, once, after a round of layoffs, one executive had 20 direct reports. That was very high for the company—most executives rarely had between three or four. From that data, it was clear that the next re-org would strike that executive's organization because that type of ratio is not sustainable. Or, that executive would get so burned out that they would leave, triggering another re-org! If and when the re-org struck, I mapped out what might happen to me and my boss. "If person A moves here, where would person B go?"

And guess what? I was often right.

This type of calculus was helpful when determining the future of the projects I was working on. *Nothing* kills projects like reorgs. If I sensed one was coming, I'd speed up the work so I could get it done, or sometimes I'd let work die if I knew that the work couldn't get done in time and I would be facing a hostile colleague or executive who'd want to kill it.

By learning to predict the upcoming changes that would impact my work at least 18 months in advance, I was able to plan my work, projects, and career.

**Choose your boss (if you can)**. There's not much else to say here other than many, many people stay in jobs they like but suffer bosses they hate. Or, they think that maybe they can make their boss like them. It'll never happen.

Sometimes, the desire to stay in a job is generational. Sometimes, there are other concerns such as family and finances. But I suggest that this staying in a bad work environment is detrimental to your mental health. You can always find another job, even if it doesn't seem like it.

**As soon as possible, discern the "professional**

**lessons" each job can teach you.** Most people just want to learn how to do their jobs. That's what I call the "day-to-day experience." This type of experience will help you be successful in the role. It might help you secure another job, especially if it's at the same company, but more often than not, your day-to-day experience is no longer relevant when you leave that job. Day-to-day experience is useful because it allows you to understand others' worldviews. As an executive mentor told me once, day-to-day experience can help you influence and work more effectively with that department in the future, if you ever work with those people again.

But there is another experience that is more valuable—I call it "universal experience." You carry universal experience with you from job to job, and it's applicable anywhere you go.

Let's take the claims adjuster profession. The day-to-day experience is learning the ins and outs of insurance policies, claims systems, and how to settle claims.

The "universal experience" you gather in claims is learning how to relate to people. By relating to many types of people, you can work more effectively and get what you want out of them. I don't mean this cynically, but practically. If, as an adjuster, you knew this on day one of the job, you would focus less on learning policy language and claims settlements and instead on trying to talk to as many different people as possible to learn what is important to them —happy people, angry people, sadistic people, parents, executives, immigrants, truck drivers, teenagers away at college, doctors, farmers, trust fund babies, and so on. Each person you talk to becomes a blueprint for the next person you meet with a similar personality. When you're at your next job and have to deal with a jerk who talks down to you in a meeting, maybe you have tools to disarm that person based on how you dealt with a similar jerk in the past.

Even though I hated my time in claims, it gave me a masterclass in learning how to work with people, even if they hate my guts.

The writing life is the same. The day-to-day experience of a writer is about learning how to write, publish, and market a book. The universal experience is learning how to communicate effectively in the written word and persuading people to take the action you want them to take: clicking your ad, buying your book after reading the book description, turning the page from the moment they read the first chapter, buying your *next* book, and so on. With fiction, it's about making people feel emotions. The universal experience of a writer is learning *mind control* through self-expression.

**Focus on professional development.** By committing to your professional development and learning, you'll remain relevant in an ever-changing marketplace.

**Do no harm.** I don't believe in hurting or backstabbing people. I've somehow managed to survive in corporate America without having to do it or having it done to me.

Let's put this all together. What does any of this have to do with personal branding for authors?

First, every day is an interview. Readers will encounter your brand 24/7/365. You must control the experience, and more often than not, this is done through metadata, search, and content such as videos, podcasts, interviews, and blog posts. Branding is everything you do. If you think about it this way, you'll think about it correctly.

Second, strive to be better than the average author. Do what others are doing, but then do things that they would never do. For example, I respond to all fan-mail. I always take the time to be thorough in my responses. Do something special and do it at a world-class level. Readers will remember. This becomes your brand.

Third, predict, predict, predict. Predict what the market

will do. Predict what other authors will do. Predict what your readers will do when they finish your books. Make predictions and update your strategy accordingly. For example, maybe there's a new type of advertising that has promise but no one is adopting it yet. That's an opportunity to create a new touch-point with a new audience.

Fourth, choose your work wisely, just as you'd choose a boss. If your writing ever becomes like a nagging boss, that's trouble. Choose the projects that you're passionate about and readers will feel it. That may not always translate into commercial success, but I'd rather be successful writing work I love than be successful writing books that make me miserable. That defeats the purpose of writing.

Fifth, focus on your professional development. Keep learning, stay committed to the craft, and keep writing, even when it's hard. Readers will remember you for being prolific, and they'll respect you for it.

Sixth, do no harm. Don't be a jerk. Don't hurt other people in exchange for your success. The publishing community is smaller than it looks, and the truth always comes out. In an era of #MeToo and social media transparency, it's much more difficult to be an asshole and get away with it. Develop a brand for being a nice author. (When I say "nice," I don't mean pushover.) That will do wonders for your author brand and help you attract more opportunities that will help you grow your business.

I distilled all of this advice into a 2-minute video, which is the main reason I decided to make this chapter so long.

# THOUGHTS ON ANIMATED BOOK COVERS

I'm seeing animated covers on the market again. Again...

I'm not a fan of animated book covers. I like how they look, but I don't like what they will lead to.

Imagine that you're browsing a book retailer and all the book covers are animated. Each cover strives to attract your attention with glitter, sparkles, flames, and kinetic wisps. It won't matter what's on the cover—all that will matter is how flashy it is.

It would be like reading *The Daily Prophet* from the *Harry Potter* series while you're trying to buy books. Yikes.

I hope book retailers resist the urge to allow animated covers. It'll just make *everything* harder for authors in a market where winning attention is already hard enough.

I see authors use animated covers on their websites and social media to add flair. Tools like Book Brush now allow you to create animated covers easier than ever before, so I don't blame people for playing around with the technology. I just hope it doesn't get abused if it goes mainstream.

# WORKING WITH APPLE

In my capacity as Outreach Manager for the Alliance of Independent Authors, I received an opportunity to work with the Apple Books team to produce a webinar called "Growing Your Sales on Apple Books." The webinar was a 45-minute presentation on why authors should distribute their books to Apple Books and how to maximize their sales on the platform. There was also a 15-minute Q&A. Suffice to say that ALLi members gained great insights into the Apple Books platform and how it differs from Amazon.

I organized the webinars and took care of the little details. The experience was a useful practice session for when I organize a future event for my community.

Here were the steps:

- I met with the Apple Books team to discuss their slides and their specific requirements. Apple has some unusual corporate guidelines, so I needed to understand those so ALLi could comply.
- I met with the ALLi team to discuss a plan for creating website pages, event calendar entries, email

communications, and social media marketing for the event.

- I locked in dates with the Apple team for two webinars, each one week apart. Because ALLi's community is international, we created one webinar for authors in the northern hemisphere and one for authors in the southern hemisphere. Around five to seven weeks from the event, we created the web pages and email communications for the event. Each event had its page, and when authors signed up, they received an autoresponder sequence that set expectations for the event. Due to Apple corporate guidelines, we could only accept 50 people on the webinar. Spots filled up in less than 24 hours.
- After the event, I sent out a survey asking authors what they thought of the event and whether they would recommend it to their friends.

There were other details, but those were the major steps. The webinars went well, and I was grateful for the opportunity.

Speaking of personal branding, you can bet that I built this experience into my resume!

# LEARNING MY LESSON ON SERIES COVERS

In the previous volume of this series, I discussed how I screwed up the design on my cover *Dead Rat Walking*. The designer was great, but I gave her instructions that led to rookie mistakes:

- I put a character against a flat background, which gave the cover no depth.
- I used a dark setting, making the hero hard to see.
- I used a dark color scheme, compounding the problem.

Again, this was not the designer's fault. I take full responsibility. But I should have known better because I made these mistakes early in my career. I thought I had learned, but apparently not.

When it was time to order the design for book two, *Rat City*, I explained my concerns to the designer and we worked to create something different that would look better in a thumbnail.

The result was more colorful and a better blend of light and dark. Is it perfect? No, but I'll take it.

It seems that I always find my design stride in the second book in a series. If the series doesn't sell well, I thought about having the cover for book one redesigned by the same designer once I finish the series. It's just an idea, but I still feel that I didn't give *Dead Rat Walking* the best chance it deserved.

Now I just need to publish the series to see what happens!

# WHY I HAVE A PRESS PAGE

For several years, I have included a "Press" page On Michael La Ronn.com and Author Level Up.com. The page showcases my public speaking highlights and lets venue organizers know that I am open to speaking engagements. It also contains a press kit with author headshots and a biography. The goal was to both promote me and make it easier for venues to feature more with less effort from me.

This quarter, my Press pages continue to reap dividends and grow my sales and brand. In one month alone, I landed two speaking engagements that specifically referenced my speaking page. The conversations started with "I saw X video on your speaking page and thought a similar talk would be great for our audience."

This is one of the rare instances where I can tell that a marketing technique is working. My Press pages took about 30 minutes each to create and cost nothing. They have provided an amazing return on investment.

# BRAVO TO A PUBLICIST

Let me start this chapter by saying that I don't recommend hiring a publicist. There's nothing wrong with the profession, but I've never seen any concrete data that a publicist can help *an indie author*. I've heard too many stories of authors spending thousands of dollars on a PR firm only to see disappointing sales. There's also the problem of fraud; there are always a few scam artists who will gladly take authors' money and provide nothing in return. You have to be careful, which is why I recommend not hiring a publicist unless you're making a lot of money and can hire a reputable firm. (Even then, I still think you're wasting money if you're not strategic about it.)

Otherwise, I don't believe publicists are practical for the everyday author. There are better, more cost-effective techniques to invest your money in.

Now that I've made my position clear, I want to take a moment to extend a bravo to a publicist.

I received an email from a publicist from Wiley (a publisher well-known for informational nonfiction, such as the *Dummies* franchise). The publicist stumbled across my YouTube channel and wondered if I would be interested in reading and reviewing an upcoming book on their roster called *Book Wars: The Digital Revolution in Publishing* by John B. Thompson. It is a historical account of the digital media revolution and how it disrupted the publishing industry. Thompson wrote a similar book in 2012 called *The Merchants of Culture*.

Not only was this book perfect for me, but it was also a great recommendation to my community. The publicist did her homework (or if she didn't, I would have never known).

I expected the book to be one-sided in its coverage, favoring traditional publishing. Quite the opposite. It not only covered the traditional publishing industry, but it also covered self-publishing in astounding detail. Thompson's research was meticulous too. It's a very academic book—not the kind you read on a Saturday night. But if you're a serious professional author like me, this book is a must-read because it gives historical perspective. Younger and less experienced writers often lack the historical perspective and there aren't many books on the history of the publishing industry, so Thompson's book is required reading.

I'm still shaking my head at the fact that a *publicist* made me aware of this book. Does it change my opinions about hiring one? No, but the experience taught me what a publicist can achieve if they do their due diligence.

# STUMBLING UPON AD IDEAS

A long time ago, I attended a Q&A session with Joanna Penn. This was before I published my first book, so it was probably in 2012 or 2013. I asked, "I can't find any comparable books similar to mine. What should I do?"

Her answer: "If you can't find a comparable book, you haven't looked hard enough."

Ouchies! Trust me, I had plumbed Amazon and Google for hours, and I could not find anything similar to the book.

Sure enough, two years later, I found a book that was comparable to mine. And it had been published well before I performed my search. For some reason, it didn't show up until then. Joanna was right.

An important lesson I've learned over the years is that you often won't find some comparable books until *years* after you publish your book.

This quarter, I was doing Amazon Ads research for my book *The Indie Author Atlas*. I happened to encounter a book called *The Writer's Atlas*, which was a book of fantasy maps. It was a perfect target for ads, yet I have no idea why I never encountered it when I was doing marketing research for *The Indie Author Atlas*. The world is funny like that.

This incident was a reminder to remain on the lookout for comparable books even after you publish your book.

# EVERYONE HAS THEIR TIME

While I wrote this book, I binge-listened to Casiopea, one of my favorite jazz Japanese fusion bands. I've been listening to them since college, but they're mostly unknown in the west except in jazz aficionado circles.

Lately, I've been watching their live concerts. They have recorded more *live* albums than most bands have *studio* albums. Their prolific live discography puts most bands to shame. Even more unusual, you can find videos of all of their live performances. It's fascinating to watch them over the years. I am captivated at how tight, consistent, and prolific they are as a band, especially between 1977 - 1988. Every year during that period, they released *at least* one album. Some years, they did two or three. Recording an album in the seventies and eighties required an extraordinary amount of manpower and planning. Only the most disciplined artists recorded more than *one* per year. Many artists during that period only recorded albums every few years. That's true today too.

At the time of this writing, the main Casiopea band recorded over 40 albums between 1977 and 2021. Its leader, Issei Noro, has recorded 17 albums under his name and various spinoff bands. The band's original bassist, Tetsuo Sakurai, has recorded 21 albums under his name as part of various spinoff bands that he created after leaving Casiopea in 1988. The bassist who replaced Sakurai, Yoshihiro Naruse, recorded nine solo albums *before* joining Casiopea. The band's (most famous early) drummer, Akira Jimbo, has recorded 34 albums under his name and as part of spinoff bands. The band's (most famous) keyboardist, Minoru Mukaiya, has recorded three albums under his name, as well as over 200 jingles that play at the Japanese train stations. Kiyomi Otaka, the keyboardist who replaced Mukaiya, recorded six solo albums before joining Casiopea.

Add the numbers up, and you have a backlist that is over 130 albums deep. That's hundreds of songs.

If you like one Casiopea album, you'll like most of them. Their style changes from album to album, but their core sound is the same. Even better, unlike many bands, the former members went on to create music that jives well with Casiopea's sound, and their solo careers are worth following.

You always know what you're going to get when you listen to Casiopea: a mixture of progressive fusion and smooth, emotional ballads. The band almost always uses a quartet configuration, but here are some ways they've changed that up over the years:

- They have rerecorded all of their classic songs with reimagined versions.
- They recorded an album where all the members play acoustic versions of their instruments.
- They recorded an album where the chord changes are almost exactly the opposite of what they would normally compose.
- They recorded an album that is best described as stadium rock meets jazz fusion.

- They recorded an album that prominently features horn sections.
- They recorded several albums that predominantly feature vocal tracks.

Yet, no matter what you're listening to, Casiopea is always a guitar, keyboard, bass, and drums. Always.

When I think about Casiopea's sound, I think about oatmeal. There are many flavors of oatmeal and ways you can eat it, but at the end of the day, it's oatmeal. That's part of the band's charm.

Consistency and a prolific work ethic lead to amazing results.

Is every Casiopea album a perfect "10"? No. Is every Casiopea song amazing? No. But with the amount of work they've produced, they have more good albums and songs than your average artist. Also, their experiments are fun to listen to, even when they don't quite work out.

As I think about writing and publishing, I don't see why this work ethic can't apply to writers. We have such a bias toward "taking ten thousand years to write a magnum opus" that prolific writers are often sneered upon. And perhaps it's a matter of preference, but I appreciate the author who writes 100 books, even if many of them strike out. Because I suspect, as is the case with Casiopea, that when that author finds his/her "tribe," they'll buy *everything*.

This is why prolific personalities fascinate me: if you start with their early works and work your way to the present day, you can see their souls in their work. You learn deep lessons about that person and their artistry that you can apply to your work in a way that you just don't get by consuming an artist who only has written one masterpiece.

Here are lessons I've learned from prolific personalities over the years:

- Quantity breeds quality.
- Never settle.
- Every artist evolves, but sometimes audiences don't like it. True courage is continuing to push in the direction you believe in.
- Being fearless comes with a career cost, but it also comes with a greater respect long-term.
- Customer tastes are cyclical; what seemed like a terrible idea decades ago will suddenly find a new life with customers.
- Today's digital age means that styles will never truly go out of vogue anymore; once something becomes popular, it may always be popular with a small group of people.
- Some ideas are ahead of their time.
- Some ideas flop tremendously.
- Every prolific artist has "good" periods and "less inspired" periods.
- Find ways to pay homage to your fans with every new work you do.
- If you enjoy the work you create, readers can FEEL it.

The key is to keep honing your craft. Are you getting better with each new book? Are you developing yourself? If you stay committed, then you'll find success in the future.

What if you found a way to think of your books like oatmeal —with each new series, you delivered something new and unique, but the core reason why readers love you remained? In other words, while the flavor might be different, the taste is similar. What would that take? What would it look like for you?

# BECOME A TECHNOLOGY
# AND DATA-DRIVEN WRITER

# THE IMPORTANCE OF BEING NIMBLE

This quarter, I fell in my driveway. I was taking my trashcan to the curb and didn't see a patch of black ice. In an instant, my cul-de-sac spiraled in front of my eyes, my hands pushed out instinctively to protect me, and my glasses went flying. I was on the ground before I even knew what happened.

It took me by so much surprise that I lay there for a few moments. My brain had to catch up with the fall.

I scraped my palms, skinned my legs, and ruined a pair of jeans, but I was otherwise okay. However, the experience got me thinking about the importance of contingency planning.

What if I had been seriously hurt? What if I had broken a wrist? What if my glasses broke? What if...?

The thought exercise led me to reevaluate my contingency plans. More importantly, though, it confirmed that I am on the right path.

I've been intentional with investing in tools and technology to help me write anywhere, in any position, and in spite of injuries.

If I had broken a wrist, I could have switched immediately

to dictation as my primary writing method, and I would have racked up *higher* word counts per session.

If my glasses broke, I could have also used dictation, probably with Dragon Anywhere, so I could at least see the screen on my phone as I spoke.

That's what it means to be nimble.

# WHY TECHNOLOGY

Since my fall in the driveway, I've been thinking a lot about technology. Technology is my number one investment. To use executive terminology, it's one of my "big bets."

I thought this chapter would be a good opportunity to recap on *why* investments in technology are important to me.

The writer of the future will be very different from the writer of today. As I look at the market, global economy, and trends, I believe that the market conditions won't always be as favorable for indie writers as they are now.

Consider this:

- Amazon will continue its monopolization efforts.
- Traditional publishers will continue to consolidate.
- Artificial intelligence will continue to drive disruption, eliminating jobs and changing the way we work. With fewer people working due to automation, they'll turn to the arts, making the "content creator economy" more crowded.
- We still don't know how COVID-19 will shape the future and customer trends.

- Traditional publishers will eventually get savvy
  about digital media and find ways to provide a
  better value for their authors, particularly through
  AI, thus making them more attractive to authors
  (but the contracts will still be terrible).

Add all of these factors together and you have an environment where today's entry and mid-level authors will find it hard to stay relevant.

The *only* way to compete in a landscape like this is through technology. Technology levels the playing field. Big companies are terrible stewards of technology; they brag as if they've mastered it, and it drives their expenses down, but talk to their employees and you'll get a different story. Plus, it's impossible to get anything done at large corporations because of bureaucracy. I say this as someone who understands the corporate world very well.

So, if traditional publishers ever get hold of effective AI, I expect that they won't truly get their money's worth out of it, even if it's making them money. That leaves a small opening for indie authors like you and me.

I'm willing to bet that if you look at the average author's workflows, they're almost all manual. This means that the author must initiate each step by hand (rather, keyboard) to accomplish them. Technology can help us eliminate manual processes.

Here's a brainstorming exercise on how technology can help us win.

- Capture your ideas using a capture service like
  Evernote or OneNote. Install these on all your
  devices. Use your phone to capture photos, audio, or

quick notes while you're out and about. Catalog your notes with tags for easy recall later.

- Use your phone to write books; write when you're on the go to bolster your daily word counts.
- Use dictation to speak your way to higher word counts.
- Invest in a writing app that does the hard work for you, such as Scrivener. When you pick the right writing app, you won't spend time fighting with it; you'll spend more time being productive.
- Use artificial intelligence to assist you with parts of your writing. Authors are experimenting with AI in helping them tell certain parts of their stories, such as randomizing planets or the weather that takes place in the story.
- Automate your editing with tools already on your computer (as I have documented with my automated editing engine).
- Invest in dedicated formatting software instead of doing it yourself. If you own a Mac, Vellum is the best app that money can buy at the time of this writing. It will save you hours of trouble with Microsoft Word. You can reinvest those hours toward writing new stories, marketing, and so on.
- Use the ONIX architecture to create a data feed that will allow you to automate your book publication and any changes. Instead of uploading a book through a dashboard, use your data feed. This is how traditional publishers do it. Outside of a couple of ebook aggregators who offer limited bulk upload, this option isn't available for indies, but the technology is. I predict this will be an option in the future.

- Use existing programming tools to help you track the health of your books and retailer product pages. How will you know if your book is pulled from sale, or if your price is wrong? You can hire someone to write software to "patrol" your properties for these sorts of events. I know because I did it!
- Write highly converting copy with a swipe file tool. (I covered this in a previous volume.)
- Write highly converting copy with an AI copywriting service.
- Use a keyword research tool like Publisher Rocket to find winning keywords and categories for your books.
- Use Microsoft Excel, Microsoft Access, or Microsoft Power BI to aggregate your sales reports into one source so that you can determine your sales. Explore this data for key insights that will inform your marketing decisions.
- Outsource less important tasks to a virtual assistant, and communicate with them using a project management tool like Slack or Asana.
- Use platforms like Upwork to hire freelancers for one-off tasks that you don't have time for.
- Use your email client's rule system to route emails to specified folders, such as expenses or royalty statements. This stops you from manually moving them, which adds up over time. More generally, triaging your emails will save time in other areas.

There are many more ways to use technology to save time, effort, and money. If you haven't yet, start investing now. You'll be shocked at how cheap it is. Almost everything you need is already on your computer.

# LIQUID TEXT

While browsing YouTube, I stumbled across a Mac app called Liquid Text. The idea behind it is novel: speed up everyday functions that a user requires with keyboard shortcuts.

For example, if you type in a word and want to look it up on Wikipedia, normally, you'd follow these steps:

- Minimize the writing app window
- Open your browser
- Go to www.wikipedia.com
- Search for the term
- Click the correct search result
- Read the page
- Minimize your browser window
- Return to your writing app

Liquid Text simplifies those steps:

- Highlight the term in your writing app
- Type Command + Shift + two to bring up the liquid search bar

- Enter the R key to bring up the reference menu
- Enter the "W" key for Wikipedia
- This will bring up the appropriate Wikipedia page
- Read the page
- Return to the writing app

While Liquid Text doesn't necessarily reduce the number of steps, it does reduce the time, mouse clicks, and effort.

It's a great idea. You can even program additional search engines into it, such as Google, Wolfram Alpha, Merriam-Webster, Dictionary.com, and more. You can even convert units if needed.

I installed Liquid Text but don't use it to its full potential. However, it got me thinking about what a fantastic tool this would be inside of a writing app.

Consider these ideas:

- Enter a keyboard shortcut to bring up a menu similar to Liquid Text that has a search engine capability, dictionaries, unit conversions, sharing, translation, advanced copy/paste, and so on.
- Access your character profiles with a key.
- Force the writing app into a certain mode. For example, in Scrivener, a keystroke will automatically create a split-screen with the current chapter on the top and the outline on the bottom. Another key will revert to your original view.
- Look up all similar instances of a word or phrase, or get statistics on how many times you've used a particular word.
- Do competitive intelligence on book retailers with a keystroke.

- Share snippets of your work-in-progress to your social media network of choice.

And more!

This could be a killer feature if a writing app developer experimented with it.

# PERFECTIT

I discovered a great proofreading add-in for Microsoft Word called PerfectIt.

PerfectIt is an app that allows you to run important proofreading checks:

- spelling and grammar
- consistent hyphenation, proper nouns, and abbreviation use
- proper table/figure numbering

And more.

PerfectIt is *not* like ProWritingAid or Grammarly. Its main function is not spelling and grammar. PerfectIt exists to make sure that your manuscript is *internally* consistent, which is often forgotten.

I bought PerfectIt within 15 minutes of using it because I understood the value. Ironically, PerfectIt isn't marketed at authors—it's marketed at editors! If editors believe in this tool enough to purchase it, then it's a worthy investment for authors.

I reviewed PerfectIt on my YouTube channel, but my audience didn't receive it well.

First, they asked what the difference was between it and Grammarly. That's my fault as I should have anticipated that objection.

Second, they resisted the subscription model. My audience *hates* subscriptions.

Third, I didn't do a good enough job explaining the benefit of internal consistency. It's a professionalism thing. Again, that was my fault.

Maybe I did a better job explaining the benefits of PerfectIt while writing this chapter, maybe not. But PerfectIt is a critical part of my editing workflow, and it has made my work considerably stronger and more cohesive. Readers won't necessarily see it, but I hope that over time, they'll feel it.

## AUTOMATOR: MOST UNDERRATED TOOL ON MAC?

For years, I promised myself that I would learn how to use the Mac's Automator app, but I kept putting it off. Not anymore.

I spent a weekend delving into tutorials on how to optimize Automator. I used it to successfully automate my bookkeeping.

I figured out how to move massive amounts of files into many different folders with just a single click.

I also figured out how to automate cleaning my desktop and downloads folders, which both get messy quickly.

Is Automator perfect? No, but it's a hell of a tool if you can find ways to use it for your needs. By understanding how to use it better, I unlocked more horsepower from my computer, which didn't cost me anything other than a few hours of my time and effort.

# KOFAX POWER PDF: GREAT LITTLE TOOL FOR PDF WORK

At work, I needed to do some advanced PDF work with a short turnaround. Because of corporate guidelines (and common sense), I'm not allowed to upload company documents to free websites that can do much of this work. That would expose company data, which would probably get me fired. My company doesn't use Adobe Acrobat because it's too expensive.

I called my IT department, and they offered to install a program that the company uses for PDF work. It was called Kofax Power PDF, which is a cheaper alternative to Adobe Acrobat.

I was impressed with it. Not only did it help me accomplish the task at hand, but it also offered a lot of cool features. I found myself playing around with it for longer than I should have. I was supposed to be working, after all!

Kofax Power PDF is also a single perpetual license, which makes it much more attractive than Adobe Acrobat. At the time of this writing, it costs $179, which isn't cheap, but it's cheaper than the $180 *per year* for Adobe Acrobat.

I don't have many uses for PDF work in my writing business, but if I did, I'd buy Kofax Power PDF without hesitation. It's available on Windows and Mac operating systems.

# THE RISE OF AI FOR COPYWRITING

Get ready for a wild ride; not this chapter, but a wave of technology that is finally hitting the self-publishing space: AI-assisted copywriting.

This technology has been around for at least a few years—I spotted it in the wild at least as early as 2018, but most people weren't investing in it. The only people using them were... (wait for it) marketers.

Now I'm seeing startups with slick products that use artificial intelligence to create highly converting copy. (Perhaps those marketers who were early adopters started these companies, but I don't know.) These startups are marketing to the average entrepreneur who hates writing copy. Most businesspeople I know don't like copywriting, authors included.

I'm seeing a shift in that influencers in the self-publishing space are covering these services now, where they didn't six months ago.

I played around with one such service, and I was impressed. I should have saved the results of my experiment, but I forgot.

The service made me fill out a questionnaire with some

details about my product and the target audience. It then produced surprisingly good copy. Some of it was obviously written by an AI, but some of it was honestly better than what I could have come up with.

The value of these services is that they can "backstop" you when you're tired or struggling to come up with converting copy. They're not a replacement for copywriting; rather, they're an assistant.

If you're interested, sign up for a free trial for one of these services and see for yourself. The results are scary good, and if they're this good now, just wait five years. Once more people adopt them, the services will build a bigger and better corpus and therefore deliver more targeted results.

One concern I do have is whether the authors that use these services will have a "sameness" in their copy. For example, are the services recommending the same taglines to all authors, or are the results truly specific to each person's project? Although minor, it's a concern.

Another concern I have is privacy. Internet marketers can't be trusted with anything, let alone our data. Remember that when you use these services (especially if they're free), that you're helping a team train their AI. This means they're gathering tons of your data, which puts them in an unfair position down the road where they control a goldmine of information that we'll have to pay to access. The services offer free trials and affordable pricing right now because they need to build a user base and accumulate more data. But what is their endgame? Is it to create amazing copywriting assistants, or is there a bigger (and possibly more sinister) goal?

Call me skeptical, but all you have to do is look at Google and Facebook to see how much power a company can gather under the guise of being helpful to people in their everyday lives.

The AI battle hasn't been won yet—there will be companies that get so rich off data and AI that they will make Google and Facebook look like Mom & Pop shops.

Skepticism aside, I do believe that AI-assisted copywriting is the future.

## HOW I SUCCESSFULLY AUTOMATED MY BOOKKEEPING

I've complained about my dislike of bookkeeping in previous volumes of this series. I don't enjoy it, but I recognize that it is critical in the event of an audit to have good books. I try to keep good records—I track all my expenses and keep all my receipts forever because you never know when you'll need them.

In 2014, I downloaded a template from the Internet that another author had compiled. It worked for a few months, but the design of the template wasn't user-friendly.

In 2015, I designed a system of my own that addressed the issues from the template I used. Here's how it worked:

- I categorized all of my expenses: cover design, editing, marketing, business, software, and so on.
- I created a corresponding folder system on my computer that matched the expense categories.
- I created a spreadsheet with tabs for each category.
- When I received an expense, I would save the PDF into the proper folder and also log an entry on the spreadsheet so that it would match the expense in the folder.

- The spreadsheet auto-calculated the categories.

This system worked well for about three years. It took me about an hour each month to categorize and organize everything, and my accountant had no issues tabulating my expenses at the end of the year for tax purposes.

However, my accountant stopped her business. I hired a new accountant who used QuickBooks. I don't like Quick-Books. The software is good at what it does, but I don't like the way it categorizes expenses. I need to be able to look at my expenses and know how they break down for *my purposes*. That said, it didn't make sense to have two systems—one for Quick-Books and one for myself.

With the new accountant, I created a new system that scrapped my categorization system. I let the accountant categorize the expenses, and I forced myself to rely on QuickBooks. I didn't like it, but it saved me time.

However, I still had the issue of saving receipts. My accountant didn't need those, but I still needed to keep records, so QuickBooks only solved part of the problem.

(Yes, I know that QuickBooks can store your receipts, but that added extra steps to my workflow.)

Using Airmail and Automator, I created a system that completely automated the cataloging of my business expenses. Here's how it worked:

- Airmail automatically flags approximately 80 percent of my expense emails and moves them to an expense folder. I move the rest manually as needed.
- I use a one-click workflow that grabs all the emails in the folder and saves them as .EML files to a designated folder on my computer. This takes approximately three minutes.

- I run an Automator Workflow that moves all of the files into proper folders accordingly based on their filenames. For example, PayPal emails have the same naming structure. This is true for all vendors I use, which makes it easy to identify the filenames with rules. This moves around 85-90 percent of the expenses automatically. I then can move the one-offs manually, which doesn't take long.
- I run a clean-up Workflow that alphabetizes everything within the subfolders.

**Total Time Before Automation**: 60 minutes per month, with 120 minutes in December for end-of-year stuff, so 780 minutes per year, or 13 hours.

**Total Time After Automation**: five minutes per month flagging and moving emails. This workflow only needs to be done once per year, so it only takes three minutes to run the Airmail workflow, one minute to run the Apple Workflows, five minutes to do remaining sorting manually, and five minutes for cleanup. Add 60 minutes per year reviewing my expenses each month to see where my numbers are. Overall, that's 79 minutes per YEAR. That's an 89 percent reduction in time spent for $0.

Is it perfect? No. I had to make some major trade-offs. But this frees up a good amount of time to do other things, and it supports my vision of having a business that runs itself.

This isn't a storybook ending, though. Turn the page to see how, despite the efficiency win, this project still ended in flames for me.

# I DON'T KNOW ANYTHING ABOUT BOOKKEEPING

Despite reducing my expense categorization process by 89 percent, I still suffered a huge failure this year. I'm sharing this because I hope that you can learn from it.

At tax time this year, I stared at an enormous "balance due" from my accountant and wondered what the hell had happened. It was a *lot* of money and I had *never* owed this much money in my life. What went wrong?

First, I hired the wrong accountant. The individual just wasn't a good fit for my family or my business.

Second, I discovered I know nothing about bookkeeping. The way that I "kept my books" was a joke. The categories I had created confused my accountant, so they slotted my expenses into their own category system based on best practices. That caused massive confusion for us both.

Third, I made some calculation errors in my spreadsheet for the year that threw off my expense count to the point where I couldn't trust my numbers. I had to go back to all my expenses and recalculate everything by hand several times to reconcile the errors. Add to the fact that I couldn't trust my accountant's numbers either.

Fourth, I waited until the last minute to do my taxes due to the pandemic, which made everything much more painful than it should have been. I never do that, but 2020 was a terrible year in more ways than one. I suppose I can be forgiven for that. But nope, I'll never make that mistake again!

Fifth, if I had known anything about bookkeeping, I could have prevented this problem entirely because I would have had a bookkeeper that took care of the expense categorization.

The episode ended well. I hired a new accountant two days before Tax Day who did a great job and shrank my balance due by two-thirds. It's amazing what a good accountant can do. I'm just bummed that I had to learn the hard way.

Anyway, I learned that my bookkeeping is a joke. Sure, I automated my *expense cataloguing*, which was great, but that didn't solve the core problem that I didn't realize I had until everything fell apart: I need a real bookkeeper. Automation can't help me with that.

Here are the lessons I learned:

- Hire the right accountant.
- Pick an expense categorization system, and never change it. Hiring the right accountant will ensure you do this correctly the first time.
- Hire a bookkeeper. Or, if you must keep your own books, take courses on bookkeeping so you can learn how to do it correctly.
- Don't delay in getting your taxes filed. Before the pandemic, I would often get mine done in February after my last 1099 arrived.
- Sit down and review your tax return. It's a pain, but you learn a lot by simply reading it. I don't know why I never did it. I'm embarrassed to admit that.

I learned what I needed to do to start preparing my business for a proper bookkeeper. I need to do a lot of cleanup, but hopefully, I'll be doing things correctly starting next year. This way, I'll be in the best possible position if I ever get audited by the government.

# BREAKING DOWN MY EDITING PROCESS

In the previous volume, I discussed my automated editing engine project. I've had the opportunity to refine it since the last volume and wanted to cover each step in the process.

First, I use Microsoft Word's spelling and grammar checker. It helps me catch at least a few errors.

Second, I use the Grammarly add-in. I've found that Grammarly does a good job of policing comma usage. It's not perfect, but good enough. Grammarly also does an above-average job of catching missing determiners, which in my opinion, are the bane of every author's existence because they're so difficult to spot.

Third, I use the ProWritingAid add-in for Word. This differs from advice I've given in the past. I ran tests on both ProWritingAid and Grammarly, and I used to recommend Grammarly for nonfiction and ProWritingAid for fiction. Most authors are on a budget and it doesn't make sense to use both. However, the more I use both apps, the more I understand their nuances and what they're especially good at. Both apps have helped me catch more errors combined than using just one. ProWritingAid is better for fiction. It also catches errors that

Grammarly does not, such as missing quotation marks. ProWritingAid can also catch some missing determiners, but not at the same rate as Grammarly.

Fourth, it's time for Word Macros. I use FREdit by Paul Beverley. FREdit is an advanced find and replace macro that can help you catch improper (but not incorrect) spelling errors, inconsistent hyphenation, and more. I can use FREdit to catch errors that my editors have recommended over the years.

Here are some examples of commands I've programmed into FREdit:

- Replace "stormwater" with "storm water"
- Replace "self publish" with "self-publish"
- Always use a comma after "Therefore" when it starts a sentence

FREdit also lets you launch other macros within it, so you can embed multiple macros within one click.

Here are some other commands I have programmed into FREdit:

- Remove multiple spaces (a common error after reviewing tracked changes)
- Highlight duplicate words ("said said" or "do do")
- Auto-insert comments based on usage rules (such as inserting a comment any time I use the word "cadence" to remind myself to use it correctly)
- Hyphenation rules based on my editor's feedback, such as replacing "wrought iron" with "wrought-iron"
- Proper noun check (it will generate a list of all proper nouns in the manuscript and color code any discrepancies)

- Italicize my book titles

Fifth, after FREdit, I have my own proprietary macros. These include:

- Numeral checks (numbers between one and ten are written out and everything higher is numericized)
- Chapter heading check (applies "Heading One" to chapter names)
- Broken link checker
- Repeat word check (looks for repeated words within a certain radius)

I run every chapter I write through this system. It takes me extra time, but it's worth it because I catch a lot of issues before the manuscript goes to my editor.

# CHAPTER SCORING FOLLOW UP

In the previous volume, I discussed a new concept that I created called "chapter scoring" as part of my editing engine project. Chapter scoring is separate from the editing process I described in the previous chapter, but it is complementary because it helps me improve my writing through data.

When I look at an editor's edits, I want to know a few things:

- How many edits did they recommend (as tracked changes)?
- How many comments did the editor make on the manuscript?
- What is the breakdown of those edits (spelling and grammar versus continuity and story)?
- How many edits did I receive per chapter?

That's a basic picture that you can glean from your edited manuscript with the right tools. You can accomplish this in seconds with automation in Microsoft Word.

The real insights are at the chapter level.

I created a tool that I called a "chapter scoring model." It sounds fancy, but it's simple: it looks at several data elements present in each chapter and then gives each chapter a score based on how well it underwent my editor's scrutiny.

The model is based on both objective and subjective factors. The data elements for the chapter scoring are:

**The total number of spelling and grammar errors.** These usually take the form of tracked changes on a Word document. These are the most important edits in the editing engine because you can teach the editing engine to spot them using code.

**The total number of continuity and story-related edits**. These usually take the form of comments in your Word document. Editors are usually hesitant to change a story issue, but they will point it out. Some comments, however, are spelling and grammar-related, so I filter out comments that don't meet these criteria. Also, I can't teach continuity edits to the editing engine. These are uniquely in the editor's territory.

**The total number of spelling and grammar-related edits and continuity and story edits**. This is perhaps the most telling number. A chapter with a higher number of total edits means it required more of the editor's attention, which is a bad sign. It's not all bad, though—you get good data and can learn a great deal!

**The number of writing sessions per chapter**. A chapter with a higher number of writing sessions may indicate more errors, especially if those sessions are spread out over several days. On the other hand, a chapter written in one session may not necessarily be better either.

**Duration of chapter creation**. If you start writing a chapter in January, suffer writer's block, and don't resume writing until March, that may indicate that more errors are present, especially of the continuity type, since it may take some time to remember the story.

**Writing method**. Some forms of writing are cleaner than others. Trust me, I would know. I find that text written by hand on my computer tends to be the cleanest, followed by text dictated while seated at my desk, followed by words written on my phone, and so on. Words I dictate using Dragon Anywhere always require the most corrections in self-editing.

These components work together within the model. For the prototype, I gave them all equal weights.

I'll share some of the hypotheses I posed while building this model because the results were insightful. I came up with these hypotheses while digging into the data and used my findings to determine whether they were correct.

**Hypothesis: The more sessions it takes to write a chapter, the more errors there will be, especially if those sessions have mixed writing methods or long lengths of time between them.**

A "session" is how many times it takes me to write a chapter.

The data showed that chapters with two or more sessions tended to have more edits, with three and four session chapters driving the highest outliers. My conclusion was that I should (try to) avoid dragging chapters out into multiple sessions wherever possible to reduce potential errors for my editor.

. . .

**Hypothesis: There is a relationship between continuity errors and spelling and grammar errors. The more continuity issues exist, the more spelling and grammar errors are likely to be present.**

The data disproved this one. There was no correlation I could find between the number of continuity (story) and spelling and grammar errors.

**Hypothesis: The longer a chapter is, the more likely it is to have errors.**

This one is intuitive. The more words that exist on the page, the more potential there is for errors. I was certain this hypothesis would be correct, but I wasn't sure how.

The data showed me that chapters higher than 2,500 words had the highest number of edits. Chapters at or lower than 1,000 words had the lowest number of edits. Longer chapters scored significantly worse.

That's insightful because I determined I could build chapter length as a special indicator of areas that need more attention. If a chapter is over 2,500 words, I can automatically flag it in the model for my editor to pay more attention to it. More practically, the data tells me that I should spend more time on longer chapters when self-editing.

**Hypothesis: The better I feel when writing, the fewer errors I will create.**

I wanted to know if mood correlated with edits. If I'm feeling great about a chapter, how does that show up in the number of edits my editor recommends? What about days where I'm feeling bad? I thought that maybe the data would give me some unique insights into writer's block.

However, the data led me down a different path. I found that the chapters where I felt "good" and "great" drove the biggest outliers of edits, which is an indicator that being in flow could cause more errors. Wow. I didn't expect that.

Two of the four biggest outliers were chapters written in flow. Even more, flow chapters contributed to approximately 25 percent of the total manuscript edits. Wow again. *One in four edits were in sections written in flow.*

This means that flow, while great for productivity, has the opposite effect on my edits. Some people might take a finding like this to mean that flow is bad. Flow is *not* bad; in fact, it's the best thing that can happen to you in a writing session. But if you hit flow and then think, "Oh crap, I'm going to have more errors," that's the danger. Fortunately, I don't think about editing when I'm writing, but others may not be able to separate the two functions. But this finding was earthshaking for me.

## Hypothesis: Some writing methods produce more errors than others.

Since I use many different writing methods, I wanted to see which one was the "cleanest."

I assumed that my laptop would be the cleanest writing method and that dictation while multitasking (through Dragon Anywhere on my phone) would be the messiest. However, the laptop drove the highest number of errors. My phone drove the lowest, but my phone contributed the fewest words to the manuscript, so that may not be true long-term.

How is it that my laptop drove the most errors? I'm staring at the screen as I write! When typing on my laptop, my writing app does not catch hyphenation or spelling issues, whereas dictation tends to catch them better. Also, I can catch dictation errors more easily because they are somewhat predictable and best caught by spellcheckers, whereas laptop errors are more difficult to detect.

## Hypothesis: A novel has fewer overall continuity errors than spelling/grammar errors.

The data showed me that this hypothesis was true. Eighty-eight percent of the total edits were spelling and grammar-related, and 12 percent of the total edits were story-related edits. Only about 40 percent of chapters received story edits.

The takeaway is that being relentless with programming any spelling/grammar edits I can find will go a long way toward reducing my overall error count.

## Hypothesis: There are more errors in the "murky middle."

This makes sense, doesn't it? The murky middle is a painful time during the writing process.

The finding? Not true. The total number of spelling and grammar and continuity edits stayed relatively stable per chapter throughout the novel. However, if I look at the scores and chunk the novel into quarters, the first and fourth quarters scored the worst. Just as mood is not necessarily an indicator of edits, neither is the "location" of the novel. The murky middle doesn't exist from a data perspective. At least that's what the data says right now.

Those were the hypotheses, and I learned a lot from them.

I shared the data with a fan in my community who is a data analyst by trade. He didn't agree with parts of my approach and helped me refine the model. For example, he felt that using components that are not inherently in the data is problematic; he thought the way I structured writing methods assumed that some methods were better than others, which was true. That's not a proper way to work with data. Additionally, he took an alternative approach with the data; he looked at each edit in terms of how many words were impacted. He assumed that each edit impacted three words on average.

His findings: "Chapters where five percent or more of the words were impacted accounted for just over half of the novel, with the worst chapter having nearly 23 percent of the words impacted and the best having less than one percent."

That's another interesting way to approach this.

Overall, the chapter scoring engine is an interesting prototype that helps me own my data and make data-driven decisions with my editing. It doesn't interfere with my writing; rather, it becomes a talking point for my editor.

# ARE YOU DATA BLIND?

Data is the future. The authors with the most data who can make the smartest insights will win.

Yet no one thinks about data in self-publishing.

Data can help you:

- understand how your books are performing and why
- figure out what books to write next
- uncover ways to sell more books
- learn how best to connect with your readers

Data can be very, very powerful.

I've been thinking about a few key questions this quarter.

- What data do I have access to?
- How can I connect data sources?
- Can I automate these connections somehow?
- Can I create a database of *all* the data I have access to?

- Can I query that database to create the reports I need?

Let me give you some examples of how these questions connect.

As an author, I have access to many sources of data: sales reports, expenses, marketing (such as Amazon Ads), Google Analytics, email marketing analytics, trackable links like Genius Link and Bit.ly, YouTube data, publishing industry statistics, to name a few.

What if, instead of viewing each data source on its own, if I wanted to connect them for better insights? For example, what if I wanted to know how much a book has "earned out" in terms of expenses? If you invested $1,000 in a book, what percentage of that have you earned back? If you advertise that book, how much are you spending, and how much money are you making on that? You can do this manually, but you can also do it in a more sophisticated way.

Other questions you might ask of your data when connecting the sources are: is there a relationship between the amount of editing you spend and your sales? How are a particular editor's edits reflected in your sales data? What about a cover designer? How many sales can you attribute to email marketing? Would it be possible to assign a dollar value to your "organic sales," ad sales, email marketing sales, affiliate sales, and more? What might that tell you about your revenue streams?

Anyway, I believe owning your data and delving into it for insights is important. You have more data than you realize—it's your job to connect it in ways that help you figure out how your author business is performing.

Are you data blind? In other words, are you ignoring the data that's all around you?

Remember, the authors with the most data and the best insights will win in tomorrow's game of publishing. Being able to own your data will become especially important when traditional publishers start adopting artificial intelligence to help them mine insights from their backlists in ways that we can't imagine.

# WHAT PUBLISHING INDUSTRY STATISTICS EXIST, AND WHAT MATTERS?

If it's not obvious by now, I've been thinking a lot about data. What kind of data do I have access to as a self-published writer? I discussed much of that data in the last chapter, but I also want to know about industry data. What is the market doing? What are other authors in my genre doing? This information is vitally important.

In other industries, we call this "competitive intelligence." In the publishing industry, authors aren't technically competing against each other, so I would consider it "cooperative intelligence." What works for one author can work for you, and you can both make a lot of money doing it. If you're successful, other authors in your genre can be just as successful without stealing readers from you, because readers are voracious. If they like your book, they'll probably want to read your author friends' books too.

In the insurance industry where I work, I have access to some great competitive intelligence tools:

- I can access public filings to see what types of products other insurance companies are filing.

- I can access stock performance, earnings reports, and other competitive data on competitors.
- I subscribe to a competitive intelligence service that sends me a daily newsletter on what competitors are doing. For example, I know early if there's a new product coming to market.
- My company has a competitive intelligence department that archives any proprietary competitor data that employees happen to find (all insurance companies do this).
- I have access to a website called AM Best that provides financial snapshots of competitors among other helpful tools.

I share all of these tools with you not because I want to geek out about insurance, but because these are exactly the type of tools that we could use in the author community. Imagine with me for a moment what proper "competitive intelligence" in the author community would look like.

Here's what I can already do today:

- I can use K-Lytic reports to obtain high-level information about certain genres *on Amazon*.
- I receive news updates from The Hot Sheet by Jane Friedman with holistic industry insights.
- I use Publisher Rocket (formerly KDP Rocket) by Dave Chesson to research keywords and ad ideas for my Amazon Ads. Other tools like this also exist and are readily available.
- I subscribe to a few publishing industry blogs that provide data on bookstore sales.
- Now, let's pretend that the following opportunities exist:

- I receive a list each morning (or week) of new titles in a particular genre. The email contains the cover, link to the book, a link to the author's website, price, book description, current sales rank, review average, retailers published at, and snippets from reviews. The same service might even allow me to download an Excel sheet with all books in a genre released in a given year. This would give me the ability to pivot, add my data, and review trends.
- I can access data on the entire publishing industry that *includes* self-publishing. I can see how sales are performing for the ebook sector, for certain genres, and for certain countries. Most data that exists right now is skewed toward traditional publishing, and it is very generic.
- I receive a weekly (or monthly) briefing that contains a digest from all the major self-publishing podcasts, blogs, and YouTube channels. Since my time is limited, I'd love a two- or three-paragraph summary of interviews. Then I can decide which content I want to explore. This would be extremely time-consuming for someone to do manually, but with artificial intelligence and advancements in natural language processing, I believe a product like this is possible within the next few years.

We'll see what types of data sources arise in the future.

Remember that traditional publishers have access to far more data than you and I. Their problem is bureaucracy and old ways of thinking; they have mountains of data, but they haven't figured out how to use it. Our problem is that we haven't learned how to own our data yet. We have to think future-forward and stay a few steps ahead of publishers—they're not our competition, but when they unlock artificial intelligence and book discoverability, they will be.

# A STORY ABOUT YOUTUBE PERFORMANCE

I discovered a "happy accident" with my YouTube channel.

I released a new video on Friday and realized that I forgot to promote it. I usually promote videos right at noon when they release, again at 1 PM, and a few tweets throughout the rest of the day.

This particular video didn't do well on the first day. It was ranked six out of ten in terms of views and watch time.

On a whim, I decided to promote the video on Saturday. I did the *same things* that I normally do: tweet on Twitter, make a Facebook post, and mention the video on my blog and YouTube community tab.

To my surprise, the video jumped from six to one in just one day. I've never seen that before. Usually, if a video languishes in the first 24 hours, it languishes forever.

The lesson? I started promoting my new videos on Fridays and Saturdays. My watch time and views jumped.

Sometimes, accidents lead to great successes.

# LEARNING PYTHON

Now that I've finished my law degree, I've decided that I want to learn another practical skill: Python.

Why Python? It's the language of artificial intelligence. It's also the most popular programming language. By learning Python, I will learn a lot.

I don't want to become a programmer. I just want to understand how a programmer thinks. I want to know what the possibilities and limitations are in code. That helps me when I'm daydreaming about new projects and chapters for this series. It's one thing to say, "I wish that X service exists," but if it's not feasible given current technology, then I'm wasting my time. It's another thing to say "I wish that X service exists" because I understand the technology and know (at a high level) how it would work. That's powerful.

Over the last year alone, I've proven this. I said that I wanted to automate my sales, and I did that using existing technology. I said that I wanted to automate editing, and I did that. So much is possible if you understand technology and data. I believe that learning Python will open up a world of possibilities for me. Hell, it might also help me get a job in the future.

I'll probably take a class at a community college or use LinkedIn Learning.

Python is a bet that I hope will pay off for me in the future. It won't cost me very much, and I'll learn a lot.

# BECOME THE WRITER OF THE FUTURE

# IF I BECAME A MEGA-BESTSELLER TOMORROW, WHAT TEAM WOULD I BUILD AROUND ME?

In my book, *Mental Models for Writers: 73 Ways to Improve Your Writing, Elevate Your Thinking, and Capture Success*, I discuss a mental model called "You are the Creative Director of Your Career," which is taken from Orna Ross, founder and director of the Alliance of Independent Authors. Orna believes that, as a self-published author, every decision is up to you. No one is going to make them for you.

If you became a mega-bestseller tomorrow, you would NOT be able to do everything yourself. You'd have to build a team around you. What would that team look like? It's an interesting thought exercise.

In the book, I wrote:

<hr />

Framed another way, you could also argue that you are the CEO of your creative career.

In a corporation, everything starts and ends with the CEO; therefore, they have to know a lot about a lot of different things.

So congratulations! You're now a CEO for the rest of this chapter!

Imagine that you're in a board room and you've assembled your C-suite for the first time.

The top executives in your writing business are staring at you, ready for orders.

Your goal is to give them instructions about how to get things done so they can carry out the day-to-day affairs of the business.

Your C-suite officers are as follows:

- Chief Marketing Officer. Where should they focus their time and what emotions do you want your books to instill in readers?
- Chief Operations Officer. How can they help your company write better books faster? What will your book covers look like? How should they find the right designers? Editors? What should the working relationships be like?
- Chief Information Officer. How will your writing business adopt new technology? How will you maximize the technology you already have?
- Chief Legal Officer. What types of publishing contracts will you sign? What happens if you get into legal trouble?
- Chief Financial Officer. How will you make money and reinvest your profits back into the business to stay sustainable?

———

After I wrote *Mental Models for Writers*, I thought of a few extra team members.

- Product Manager. This person would patrol book retailers regularly to spot errors such as typos in book descriptions, incorrect prices, and so on. They would also be responsible for updating the packaging.
- Administrative Assistant. This person would help me with emails at scale and possibly oversee a team of admins who serve various purposes.
- Programmer. I'd keep a developer on retainer for items on my website that need to be done.
- Media Professional. This person would make me look good and sound good as well as edit my audio and video.
- Personal Stylist. Call me vain, but if you reach mega-bestseller status, your looks will be scrutinized. This person would make sure that I'm always looking good for the camera.
- Accountant. This person would be on retainer and report directly to the CFO. They'd do my taxes and help me minimize my tax liability.
- Financial Investor. This person would help me manage my financial investments and assets.

Here's the thing. It was a fun thought exercise to imagine this team. The responsibilities I listed are damn near what an author's job description should be. Turn the page to read more about that.

# AN AUTHOR'S JOB DESCRIPTION

I also wrote this in *Mental Models for Writers:*

━━━

When I was a manager in corporate America, I had to hire people. Hiring comes with a ceremony of many rituals, one of which is writing a job description for the role you're hiring for.

Job descriptions serve as reminders to employees and bosses about what the employee is supposed to do. In many cases, it's also an important legal document.

If you were going to write your job description as an indie author, what would it look like?

- What are the core elements of your job?
- How will you divide your time between those core elements?
- How will you handle the non-core elements? Will you simply not do them, or will you outsource them?

- How will you assess yourself to gauge your progress? In other words, how will you know if you're doing a good job?
- How often will you reassess your priorities?
- What are your "other duties as assigned"? Do they take up more of your time than they should?

When you write your job description, it forces you to think hard about the limited time and resources you have.

For example, I have discovered over the years that I'm an idea guy. I like to conceive ideas and build stuff (such as books, videos, and courses). But when it comes to maintaining the things I build, I'm not good at it because it's not my passion. Some people are the exact opposite—they want nothing to do with idea generation or building a product, but they enjoy maintaining something, making rules, enforcing those rules, and contributing to a community.

My job description would focus on content creation and engaging with people in my community around my ideas. It would not include a Facebook community, for example, because I don't have the energy or patience to run a group like that. At the end of the day, it's my career, and I'm going to do it my way.

Remember: it's your career.

---

Let's have some fun with a job description based on the "mega-bestselling team" I built around me in the last chapter.

## JOB DESCRIPTION FOR A SELF-PUBLISHED AUTHOR

. . .

The self-published author provides their strategic direction about the types of books they want to publish. This position is responsible for strategic leadership, content production, and overseeing every process of publication. It also proactively participates with editors, cover designers, and other freelancers to accomplish projects and meet business objectives.

- Writes amazing books.
- Manages existing books and content and ensures they are always up-to-date and effectively marketed.
- Identifies target audiences and the best ways to market books to them.
- Aggressively pursues new marketing opportunities and manages ad campaigns to drive revenue and growth.
- Finds new ways to produce content faster and more effectively, leveraging technology and automation.
- Collaborates regularly with editors, cover designers, and other freelancers.
- Responsible for all legal contracts.
- Oversees the business and manages the day-to-day financial operations.
- Responds to emails and fan-mail promptly.
- Updates website as necessary.
- Produces audio and visual content to support the author brand.
- Actively supports the self-publishing community through mentoring other authors.
- Pursues continuing education to continue honing the craft.
- All other duties as assigned.

That, in my opinion, is a multimillion-dollar job description!

I don't know about you, but when I list all of these responsibilities on paper, it makes me truly understand how desperately outsourcing is needed in our community, yet most authors can't afford it. In a previous volume, I wrote about how authors can pool their money to make virtual assistant services affordable. I believe that is a winning strategy.

This description also shows you that it is unacceptable *not* to outsource once you start making real money with your writing. There just isn't enough time in the day.

What I've done over the years is to look at this job description and determine my priorities. Pick your top five, focus on those, and do the rest when you can. You already know my top five:

- Become a world-class content creator
- Become a world-class marketer
- Become a technology-driven writer
- Become a data-driven writer
- Become the writer of the future

I spend at least 80 percent of my time in these areas.

What does *your* author job description look like?

# FOLLOWING AN EDITOR'S
# CAREER PATH

Authors work with editors regularly. Aside from cover designers, editors are the most frequent freelancer that authors work with.

In the last chapter, I discussed the author's job description. What about an editor?

More importantly, what does an editor have to do to become an editor? As executives in the corporate world would say, "What's the career path?"

Does an author have a career path? Not really. Usually, it involves reading a ton of books as a kid and then waking up one day and saying that you want to be a writer. The moment you write your first book, the career pathing is done. After that, it's about developing yourself.

Editing is different. A good editor goes through some level of training, either by sheer experience or by taking classes.

I don't care if an editor has a college degree or if they've worked for a publishing house. I also don't (necessarily) care about their years of experience, as long as my manuscript isn't the first one they've ever worked on. I just care about the result. And I know what a good editing product looks like after working with around a dozen editors in my career.

What would it be like to step into an editor's shoes? What if, to understand our editors better, we said, "Let's follow the career path of an editor"?

That's fascinating to me. The only problem is that there is no uniformity. There's no "editing school." Every editor's experience is different. But what do many editors have in common?

I saw some training courses on the American Copyeditors Society (ACES) and the Chartered Institute of Editors and Proofreaders (CIEP) in the UK. These are societies dedicated to cultivating editing talent. They offer memberships, training classes, and other resources to help editors become better editors and find work. If anyone would know what an editor needs to learn to become competent, it would be ACES and CIEP. (If you don't live in the US or the UK, check if your country has an editing society. They probably do.)

Here are titles of classes from the ACES Academy website at the time I wrote this article:

- Microaggressions in Editing: Understanding Biases in Editing and Undoing Harm
- How to Master the Business Side of Editing
- Respect: How Editors and Writers Build Great Relationships
- Let's Get Technical: How to Plan and Edit Content About Technology
- When Words & Design Collide: How to Write and Edit with Design in Mind
- Perspectives: People of Color in the Editing Community
- What's New in the APA Style
- The Invention of the Modern American Dictionary

- Grammar Arcana

When I checked the CIEP website, I found a jackpot: a document called "Curriculum for Professional Development" for editors.

Here's what the curriculum contains:

- Professional practice and ethics
- Business management and practice
- Equipment and file management
- Production knowledge and practice: workflows, schedules and budgeting, editorial processes, production processes, design, typography and typesetting, printing and finishing, ebook formats, tables and illustrative materials, different models of publishing, principles of accessibility, and so on
- Editorial knowledge: grammar, punctuation, usage, spelling, voice and tone, citations, references and bibliographies, numeracy, use of languages, sources of information, indexing, and so on
- Editorial judgment
- Editorial practice: markup, editorial standards in context, errors, omissions and other problems, house style, project style sheets, and so on
- Specialist skills in knowledge: medical, technical, legal, music publishing, and so on.

This list is interesting. From comparing the ACES class list and the CIEP curriculum, we can say at a high level that an editor's career training would contain:

- Professional practice and ethics: how should an editor conduct themselves?

- Business: How should an editor conduct their business, market themselves, and price for their services?
- Equipment and file management: How should an editor archive writers' documents? How should they protect their writers' data?
- Editorial knowledge: How can an editor rapidly improve their knowledge of the rules of English and its style manuals?
- Editorial judgment: How should an editor learn to think like an editor and challenge inherent assumptions in a work?
- Editorial practice: What are the best practices for how an editor should mark up a manuscript and conduct communications with writers?
- Specialist skills: What areas should an editor specialize in, and what are the rules of those special areas?
- Equity: How can an editor ensure that an author's work is free of implicit bias?
- Technology: How can editors become masters of the software they use?

With this curriculum in mind, if you wanted to understand editors better, just take appropriate classes and talk to editors about the different items. Pretend that you're going to become an editor, even though you'll never edit a single manuscript.

Let's run through this list again and discover the benefits we can learn by learning to think like an editor. Imagine that you are searching for a new editor and you're evaluating someone who seems like a good fit.

- Professional practice and ethics: Is this person conducting themselves according to industry standards?
- Business: Is this editor underpricing or overpricing their work? Are they a competent business person? Are their contracts fair?
- Equipment and file management: More generally, how might this editor store their documents? Is there something I can learn about this to store documents more effectively in my writing business?
- Editorial knowledge: Is the editor competent at editing? (I know, I know...it's shocking how little knowledge of spelling and grammar factors into this curriculum, but that's true of the writing profession too.)
- Editorial judgment: Will this editor help me improve the clarity in my work?
- Editorial practice: How does this editor prefer to work?
- Specialist skills: Does this editor specialize in my book's genre or subject matter?
- Equity: Does this editor have the proper knowledge to help me avoid implicit bias in my work that might be distracting to readers?
- Technology: Is the editor competent at Word?

Some of these questions are basic, but others can help you to truly understand the editing profession. Considering that most writers want to be writers for a long time, it only makes sense to understand your editor.

Now that I'm done with law school (which I'll discuss in the next chapter), I've been thinking about exploring the editing career path for my own knowledge.

# LESSONS LEARNED FROM LAW SCHOOL

In May 2021, I finally graduated from law school. It took me four and a half years, but only because I had to take a couple of semesters off for personal reasons. I probably could have finished in three years.

My degree is a specialized Master's in risk management and compliance. It's insurance-focused.

Law school is an amazing experience. I didn't get the "full" experience, though—I only took one class at a time in the evenings, but I was just as busy, if not busier than your average full-time law student. I was raising a toddler, working 50 hours a week as a manager at a Fortune 100 insurance company, taking law school classes, traveling the state and teaching insurance classes, writing books at a prolific pace, hosting three podcasts, running a YouTube channel, doing public speaking engagements, and managing a video editor.

I look back at the last five years and wonder how the hell I did it.

I admit to people all the time that law school slowed my productivity down immensely.

I attended law school between the fall of 2017 and the spring of 2021. During that time:

- I wrote 26 books (11 novels and 15 writing books).
- I recorded around 700 podcast episodes for all of my podcasts combined.

Most people would read those numbers and say, "What do you mean law school slowed you down???"

For each class (at least in the beginning), I spent approximately three to six hours per week in class, and an additional three to six hours a week studying. If I'm honest, I studied much, much less after the first year, but hey...

That's 12 hours per week dedicated to just law school.

I've analyzed my writing output over the years and I've learned that it takes me approximately 40 hours to write, edit, and format a novel.

Twelve hours per week for 12 weeks is 144 hours, which equals 3.6 novels per semester. That's how many novels I could have written during that semester in a perfect world.

I attended law school for seven semesters, so that's a net loss of 25 novels during my time there. I've written around 60 books now, so if I hadn't gone to law school, it's not insurmountable that I could have had *around* 85 books to my name at the time of this writing.

I could do some more math about how much each of my novels earns me, and you would see how much time and long-term money I lost throughout my career. It's a *big* number. It's akin to cashing out your retirement investments before you retire—it doesn't seem like a lot of money, but you're missing out on the future value of your money.

That begs the question of why even go to law school? I just explained that I lost an incredible about of time and money, and that I robbed myself of the ability to write books that I would have enjoyed. Also, I did not go to law school to be an attorney, and I will never practice law because my degree doesn't allow me to.

Huh???

I went to law school to improve my knowledge and professional development. I wanted to learn how to "think" like a lawyer, how to use that knowledge to avoid legal pitfalls in my writing business. Also, because the degree is technically a Master's degree, that provides me more earning power in my professional life. I also attended because I enjoy legal studies and thought it would be interesting.

I went because my employer paid for 95 percent of it. I just had to pay for books, which was around $200 each semester. I graduated debt-free.

I spent about $1,400 on the degree out of my pocket. Just having the degree on my resume helped me land three different jobs while I was in law school, including a new job as an executive one month before graduation, which resulted in a salary increase well above the $1,400 that I invested. The degree produced a very good ROI for my career.

Here are the lessons I learned from law school.

- I can handle a lot of pressure. I already listed the concurrent activities I managed while attending school. There were a few points where I exceeded my capacity, but ultimately, I thrived under the high pressure. I emerged from law school without any substance abuse issues, with my marriage still intact, and with a promotion at work. My appetite for risk and high pressure is higher than most people's, and I've learned that it serves me well.

- I learned how to read (and negotiate) contracts like a lawyer. One day, if I'm ever staring at a film deal or a licensing agreement, I'll know how the terms will impact my career, and most importantly, I'll know when to call a lawyer.
- I took Employment Law. The information will be very, very helpful when it's time to hire people full-time into my writing business.
- I took Copyright Law. Since authors make their money off copyright, this class was worth the cost of the degree alone.
- I have a knack for spotting opportunities that others overlook. A "Masters" law degree is usually a laughingstock of the law community. No one in the legal profession takes you seriously. I knew this before I even applied. Yet I had no desire to practice law and knew that the degree, while not helpful in the legal world, would help me immensely in the corporate world. This type of degree is still so new that corporate people have no idea what a law degree in risk management and compliance is—they just see the law school on my resume and that I have a law degree. I don't hold myself out as a lawyer and never will, but just by having this degree, my portfolio looks different to recruiters and hiring managers because most people at my level have MBAs. I think MBAs are boring and would have never attended school for one. I knew that this unique law degree could become a talking point in interviews and I could sell it. Plus, it's good insurance if I ever get laid off because I have a Master's level degree. Additionally, I knew that the degree would benefit my writing business. I knew

all of this before pursuing it. I'm proud of myself for recognizing these opportunities, and it paid off.

Now that I'm done with law school, I suddenly have 12 hours per week that I can devote to my writing again. I'm excited about that. I got what I needed out of the experience, and now it's time for the next thing, whatever that may be. But one thing is clear: I'm done with traditional education and will not be spending any more time or money toward degrees.

# LESSON FROM A SHAOLIN MONK

This quarter, I stumbled upon a TED Talk that encapsulates almost every problem new writers have. It so neatly sums up the problems that I hear from writers weekly that I wanted to share and summarize it. The talk is given by a Shaolin monk, Master Shi Heng Yi.

Writing is about knowing and mastering thyself. Master thyself and you master your surroundings. Master Shi Heng Yi speaks about this:

"To bring meaning to your life
to bring value into your life
you need to learn and master yourself and
don't let the hindrances stop you."

In his TED Talk, Master Shi Heng Yi discusses the Five Hindrances to Self-Mastery.

**#1: Sensual desires**. Master Shi Heng Yi refers to this as anything you can experience in the five senses: touch, sight, taste, smell, and hearing. He uses the example of climbing a mountain and suddenly discovering that there is an amazing restaurant carved into the mountainside. The smell of the delicious food lures you off track, and you stop to eat in the restaurant. You never leave because it is comfortable and you can't imagine climbing the mountain when you're in the pleasure of delicious food and good company.

To put this into context:

- Many writers in the community come for the writing but stay for the community. They talk about writing and enjoy other writers' company, but they don't ever get around to writing.
- Many writers in the community seek out everything there is to learn about writing but never get around to writing.

**#2: Ill will/aversion**. Master Shi Heng Yi refers to this as discomfort. If you're climbing the mountain and it starts raining and you don't have an umbrella, you turn around and go home. But the rain is exactly what you need to temper your spirit. Just because it's uncomfortable doesn't mean you should stop; it means you should keep going. Seeking comfort means missing out on clarity.

To put this into context: how many people start writing but quit because it's too hard? How many people finish their first book but never publish it? How many people publish their first book and quit because the marketing is too hard? How many people publish several books and quit because of lack of success? Writing is expensive, time-consuming, and draining, and if all you can see are the negative parts, you'll miss out on so much.

**#3: Dullness/heaviness**. Master Shi Heng Yi refers to this as your mind being locked in a cell. You tell yourself you can't write well, or you fall for the movies your critical voice plays inside your head. What you don't realize is that while you *appear* to be locked in a cell, the door is unlocked and you can leave at any time. You just have to have the courage to do so.

To put this into context, read anything I've written about self-doubt. I talk about how so many writers get trapped in the theaters of their minds. They tell themselves they can't do something, or that their writing isn't good enough, or (insert any excuse). It stops them from making progress.

In my opinion, this is the biggest problem that writers face. Everyone, without exception, gets locked in a cell for a time. Not everyone escapes, though. I've been locked in the cell many times, but never for long.

**#4: Restlessness**. If you're too focused on the future or the past, you cannot be focused on the present. You cannot enjoy your writing journey or appreciate where you are. That's deadly.

To put this into context: so many writers want to be rich overnight. They want to write one book and become immensely successful. Everyone wants notoriety yesterday, and they're in a hurry to get it. Who doesn't want more book sales?

Instead, could you focus on where you are right now and be appreciative of it? Sure, it may not be where you want to be, but every time is a special time, and there's always something to appreciate about where you are in your journey, even if you don't have an audience.

**#5: Skeptical Doubt**. This is self-doubt. If you doubt yourself, then nothing is possible until you set those doubts aside. The scary part about self-doubt is that it's the last hindrance that Master Shi Heng Yi talks about, the last one before you reach the mountaintop.

To put this into context: so many writers are closer than they think to the next level of their writing career. They just have to have the courage to keep going. The closer they get to the summit, the louder the "skeptical doubt" (self-doubt) gets.

. . .

## FACING THE HINDRANCES

Whenever you face a hindrance in your life, Master Shi Heng Yi recommends a four-step process he calls "letting it R.A.I.N."

1. Recognize the hindrance. Figure out how you are feeling in response to it, and where those feelings are coming from.
2. Accept the situation. Hindrances never go away completely; understanding their nature and accepting it is key to defeating them.
3. Investigate. Ask how you got yourself to this point. What will you do about it, and how can you avoid this next time?
4. Non-Identity. If you believe in Hindu philosophy, it's the same as "being attached and unattached at the same time." Separate yourself from your body and set your emotions aside. Then keep going.

I could explain more about Master Shi Heng Yi's philosophy, but you should check it out. I find it amazing how nonwriting philosophers and spiritual guides offer advice that applies to writing.

Master Shi Heng Yi's talk offers the answer to every writing problem that exists if you're willing to listen.

The big one is dullness/heaviness. Just because you're locked in a cage doesn't mean you can't get out. No one can hold you. Remember that the door is always unlocked.

# TOM CRUISE DEEPFAKE

Earlier this year, a video of a Tom Cruise deep fake went viral. It shows footage of Tom Cruise talking to the camera, but it's not Tom Cruise.

Watch the video; it's eerie and disturbing at how far deep-fake technology has become. Many experts are calling the Tom Cruise video a watershed moment for the technology.

If you're an influencer, that should scare you.

Why Tom Cruise? He's a celebrity and there is a *lot* of footage of him. The guy has made tons of movies and given hours and hours of interviews. Artificial intelligence needs copious amounts of data, and that data exists for Cruise in the form of videos that probably total hundreds of hours.

Guess who else has lots of videos that can easily be down-loaded for free to create deepfakes? Influencers!

My YouTube channel alone has over 300 videos. I'm the only subject in the frame for most of my videos. Someone could create a deepfake of me easily. This is true of many YouTubers, especially as the technology becomes more sophisticated and needs fewer video data to be effective.

The concern many people have about deepfakes is that

we're headed for a world where it's hard to know what is truth and what is fake, deception, or misinformation. Imagine a deepfake of a president or world leader saying something that incites war, or a "sex tape" with an influencer's face on a model that looks real. (This already exists, but the results look fake.)

Technology doesn't yet exist to "spot" deepfakes, and if it doesn't come to pass, that's scary.

Influencers are a target, and I believe it will be a good idea for influencers to think about how they can protect themselves against the threat of deepfakes. They should have a plan in place about what to do if they find themselves the victim of a deepfake that threatens their career. They should communicate that plan with their fans too. The future might usher in the rise of two-factor authentication for influencer content; an influencer might upload a video to a site like YouTube, but they would also publish a certificate of authenticity on their website so that if the video doesn't match the certificate, then it gets flagged. This way, someone can create a deepfake, but additionally, they would also have to hack the author's website. This would only protect an influencer for the content they personally create, though. If a difficult future unfolds where people cannot determine the veracity of videos, I can see some influencers restricting appearances to their official channels or the channels of people they trust to prevent potential deepfakes.

Technically, YouTube's Content ID system can flag videos that infringe copyright. I suppose that the technology could be evolved to spot deepfakes too.

But I'm not an alarmist. I also believe that deepfake technology has great promise for writers:

**Cover designs with people of color**. Writers who want to put a person of color on the cover have a major problem right now: it's difficult to find suitable models of color. For example, when I was searching for a model for my *Magic Trackers* series, I needed a strong African-American heroine. My designer and I searched royalty-free photo sites such as Shutterstock and Canstock, and we only had a few options. We needed a model who had many different poses; we found that many of the models only had a handful of poses, and not all of those were suitable for a book cover. Deepfakes can eliminate this issue by creating models of color that are a composite of many different models. You simply pay the models whose images are used to create the composite, and you'd do this through Blockchain and cryptocurrencies.

**Character art**. Currently, it is expensive to create character art. You have to find a designer. Imagine deepfake technology that makes a composite of multiple artists' work to create character art that you can share with your fans. You could even do this with photography. Want a hunky twenty-something male leaning against a motorcycle in a dark alley? You got it!

**Author photos**. Imagine a deepfake program that can review every photo ever taken of you and create a composite author headshot that never actually existed. You'd never have to worry about taking headshots ever again, and you could just update them every few years, and your headshots would age with you.

So the technology is not all bad. Like any emerging issue, it's up to us to decide if it will be good or evil.

# Q2 PROGRESS REPORT

In the previous volume, I shared the progress I was making toward my 2021 author strategy. This strategy will guide me for the next several years. I wanted to provide an update for Q2 2021.

## MY STRATEGY

My mission is to educate and entertain my audience in the genres I write, and to remain nimble in an ever-changing industry.

I will achieve my mission through five strategic priorities:

- Become a world-class content creator
- Become a world-class marketer
- Become a technology-driven writer
- Become a data-driven writer
- Become the writer of the future

## WORLD-CLASS CONTENT CREATOR

**Goal: 64 books published by 12/31/2021.** I'm currently at 55 books written (including this one). That means I need to write nine more books this year. I'm in danger of missing my plan, so I'll need to do another "beast mode" challenge in Q3 to catch up.

**Develop a way to ensure consistency across my platform**. This is just a fancy way of saying that I need to ensure that my work is consistent and that readers are receiving a consistent experience. In the Q1 update, I said that my editing engine was part of this initiative because it will go a long way toward ensuring a better reader experience. To date, I have not yet thought about other ways to do this across the rest of my platform.

## WORLD-CLASS MARKETER

**Grow my Amazon Ad imprint.** My sales continue to rise from my use of Amazon Ads.

**Improve my copywriting skills.** The sales copy builder I created continues to work well for me. I even used it to write a book description for a family member who is making his debut self-published poetry collection this year.

**Reduce my tax liability.** I made progress in this area and then suffered several steps backward. That said, my knowledge of tax law is substantially improved compared to last quarter due to the tax debacle that I described in this volume.

## BECOME A TECHNOLOGY-DRIVEN WRITER

**Develop an automated way to enforce consistency.** My editing engine project this quarter satisfies this requirement. All of my manuscripts now go through it before sending to my editor.

**Redesign my Book Wizard tool on Michael La Ronn.com and** "Author Level Up".**com**. Still no progress on this goal. It'll be a focus in Q3 and Q4.

**Implement a flexible book database that houses all the metadata for my books.** Still no progress here. I may punt this to 2022.

**Automate my bookkeeping.** I've talked enough about this topic in this book that I don't need to cover it anymore here, but I satisfied this goal.

## BECOME A DATA-DRIVEN WRITER

**Make minor enhancements to my sales database**. No progress.

**Invest in learning the basics of Python, Webhooks, and Application Programming Interfaces (APIs).** This is good knowledge to understand for the future. I'll probably sign up for a class starting in Q4.

## BECOME THE WRITER OF THE FUTURE

**Read 50 books.** I'm about 50 percent toward the goal, with around 20 books read this year.

**Implement direct print and audiobook sales on my website.** No progress here yet, but I do have an audiobook distributor lined up.

**Complete my law degree.** Completed.

**Complete 12 WMG workshops to improve my writing craft.** I'm in danger of missing this goal. I'll have to make it a focus in Q3 or Q4.

. . .

## BRINGING IT ALL TOGETHER

My final law semester and my new job put a dent in my goals for the year, but I'm still making progress.

The editing engine is a gigantic win, and I should still hit my book production goals, even if I fall behind.

I'll have to focus on the other goals in the upcoming quarters. My goals are solely my own; no one will die if I don't achieve them, but I'd like to have a killer goal year this year so that I can start reducing my goals in future years. I've benefited from my investments in production, technology, and data, so I don't need to be so aggressive with goals moving forward.

I'll share more progress on my strategy in the next volume so I can keep myself accountable, but you can view the details of my 2021 + strategy by visiting www.authorlevelup.com/2021strategy.

# IDEAS YOU CAN STEAL

# OPEN-SOURCE COMPUTER VISION IDEA

Computer vision is a type of artificial intelligence that recognizes images. A classic example of computer vision is the lane detection technology in automobiles; the car can detect the lane and notify you when you accidentally change lanes without your turn signal on.

Advancements in computer vision have implications in every area of our lives. This is also true in publishing.

What if you could train computer vision software to identify book covers?

I was doing some competitive intelligence on the urban fantasy genre on Amazon. If you've ever browsed bestseller lists on Amazon, then you know that it's an exercise in frustration. Authors frequently misclassify their books to get visibility. It's not uncommon to look at, say, an urban fantasy bestseller list, and see it overrun with titles that aren't even urban fantasy. But I digress.

Computer vision is object recognition. Just imagine what software could do when the answers to the questions below are YES:

Can it detect urban fantasy covers?

Can it detect subgenres of UF? Such as cozy mystery?

Can it detect the gender?

Can it detect hair colors?

Can it detect emotions on a character's face?

Can it detect magic?

Can it detect objects such as swords?

Can it detect fonts?

Can it detect colors on the cover?

A book cover is just an assembly of symbols. Computer vision can and should be able to read book covers easily.

What if someone created computer vision software that crawled book retailers and identified books based on genre? What if it could detect urban fantasy covers, sort those covers into subgenres, and then pass that data to a report, such as some of the ones I mentioned earlier in this volume? Imagine receiving a report in your inbox that says, "Per your request, here are newly published urban fantasy detective novels about werewolves." Wow.

Why would you care about this? Let me tell you a story. In 2019 , I released a series called *The Good Necromancer*. It's about an ex-necromancer named Lester Broussard who made a pact with a demon that went wrong, and the demon killed his family. Ridden with guilt and shame, he's trying to live a normal life and atone for his sin. When an old friend asks him for help, he finds himself delving back into the dark art of necromancy.

When I wrote *The Good Necromancer*, there weren't many urban fantasy novels featuring necromancers. I only found three series that were comparable to mine.

But what happens if necromancers become hot five years from now? I want to know when that happens! A service like the one I described would ensure that I stay up-to-date with any necromancer novels that are published after mine. This way, I can run ads toward the new books, collaborate with those authors, and figure out what readers like about the new books. Maybe I'd need to update my covers or book description to adapt to a new trend.

When you have as many books as I do, you simply cannot keep track of what is happening on the market. I've written in around a dozen genres—I can't research all of those genres all of the time. A tool like this fills in a critical gap that prolific authors need.

# THOUGHTS ON MENTORING: AUTOMATED MENTOR SELECTION AND REVERSE MENTORSHIPS

I obtained a new mentor this year in my professional life, and the experience got me thinking about mentorships in the author space.

The company I worked at had a prestigious program where you had to fill out an application that was reviewed by the Office of Human Resources, and they assigned you a mentor at least one level above your title based on your goals. The mentor also filled out an application so there was a detailed matching process.

Because of expense reductions, the company hired a vendor who automated the mentor matching process. The entire process worked without a single human involved.

Here's how it worked:

- I set up a profile and filled out an application that detailed my goals.
- Based on my answers, the program showed me a list of mentors it thought would be a good match.
- I reviewed the mentor's profiles and picked my top three candidates; the mentors did the same thing.

- The system matched you based on preference.
- Both the mentor and mentee received an automated email explaining the process and expectations.

I was skeptical. In the corporate world, any time the company brings in a "vendor" to do something that used to be someone's job, the results are almost always lackluster. This program was one of those rare exceptions.

I was matched with a mentor who, quite frankly, was like a kindred spirit. She had the same level of ambition as me, and she was only a year older than me. However, she was a director and I was a manager.

We were a great match and I learned a lot from her.

That got me thinking about why we can't have something like that in the author space.

A few years ago, the Alliance of Independent Authors facilitated a similar program using Facebook. I was a mentor through that program.

I believe a website that matches successful authors with author mentees would be effective. Authors tend to be shy, and in the digital age, it's not exactly easy to approach someone you don't know to ask them to be a mentor. A website like this removes friction because both parties are willing to participate.

I wouldn't be surprised if something like this doesn't already exist, but I haven't seen anything specifically for authors.

The second thought I had around mentorships was around reverse mentorships. I've heard of mentorships where the mentor-mentee relationship is the opposite: the mentor is the junior employee and the mentee is the senior employee. For example, an executive might want to learn more about a particular business unit, so they enlist an entry-level employee to help them learn. The entry-level employee also gains the benefit of working with a more experienced employee. I also don't see why this can't apply in the author world.

Bestselling authors and more experienced authors lose touch with emerging trends. Today's hot new authors will inevitably be tomorrow's opponents of new processes and technology. I'll bet money on it. Although new authors lack experience in publishing, they contain a wealth of information. Publishing a book in 2021 is vastly different than 2012. The marketing tactics are also different. An experienced author can learn a lot from newbies, even if the newbies aren't successful in their endeavors.

While I have experience as an author, I still think of myself as a newbie. But as the years go on, it makes a lot of sense for me to establish a reverse mentorship. The person I'd like to learn from probably hasn't graduated high school yet, honestly.

I want to be "forever young" when it comes to publishing. I want to capitalize on new trends to reach new readers, and I want to make sure that my books are always speaking the language of relevance. A reverse mentorship can help with that.

## GENRE-SPECIFIC BOUTIQUES

I've said for a while that when you're hiring freelancers, it's best to hire someone who has experience in your genre (if you can). Assuming the same level of competence, an editor who has extensively edited in your genre is almost always better than an editor who has not. The same is true with cover design.

I see value in a "boutique" that only services authors of a certain genre.

For example, you could hire an "urban fantasy boutique" whose editors and cover designers specialize in urban fantasy. When you work with them, you're guaranteed to create packaging that will be relevant for urban fantasy readers because the freelancers specialize in it.

There are economic reasons why this might not work, namely scale. Most freelancers are generalists because they might only edit a few manuscripts in a certain genre a year. But a boutique service could work well for successful authors or newbies with means who are willing to invest in a higher level of quality.

Imagine hiring a firm that would:

- Assign you an editor and cover designer who specializes in your genre
- Provide genre-specific marketing services and advice
- Update you about trends in the genre

This is almost like a traditional publisher, but they don't take your copyright. You simply pay them for their proven expertise.

# 80/20 YOUR 80/20

I picked up this idea from James Altucher in his new book *Skip the Line*.

Altucher discusses the 80/20 rule (also known as the Pareto Principle), which says that 80 percent of results come from 20 percent of the causes. For example, if you write 100 books, 20 of those books will drive 80 percent of your income.

Altucher's idea is to 80/20 your 80/20 results. In his reasoning, if it's true that 20 books will drive 80 percent of your income, then it might also be true that 20 percent of those 20 books will drive 80 percent of that 80 percent. It's a very meta idea, but the gist is that instead of focusing on 20 books that drive your income, you should focus on four. If you put your energy into those four books, you'll reap the benefits faster.

This is a fascinating idea because you can apply it anywhere the 80/20 rule applies.

## IDEAL DAY

What's your ideal day as a writer? After reading Bertrand Russell's *The Conquest of Happiness*, I thought about what mine would look like. I wrote down my thoughts and I'm inviting you to think about your ideal day as a full-time author.

I'd wake up at 5:30 AM to exercise, eat breakfast, and get an early-morning writing session in.

At 7:30 AM, I'd leave to take my daughter to school.

At 8:00 AM, I'd return home and start writing again.

At 11:30 AM, I'd eat lunch, get another workout in, take my dog on a nice long walk, and watch some YouTube videos.

At 1:00 PM, I'd sit down and work on business and marketing items.

At 2:00 PM, I'd devote the rest of the afternoon to reading and consuming content.

At 4:00 PM, I'd pick my daughter up from school. Then it would be dinner time and family time.

At 8:00 PM, I'd spend more time reading and preparing for the next day.

At 9:00 PM, I'd go to bed.

On a perfect day like this, I'd probably write anywhere from

3,000 to 5,000 words. That's 21,000 to 35,000 words per week, 1.82 million words per year, and a whole lotta fun writing!

Not every day would be the same, and I'd weave in other tasks such as podcast interviews, research for a new book, or simply running to the post office if I need to do that. My day would be structured around whatever I need. If my daughter is sick, I can take a day off. If I need to go to a doctor's appointment, I can take an afternoon to do that. And despite what I do, the words continue to add up, the money continues to hit my bank account on schedule, and my happiness is unbound. I suppose this is the definition of freedom.

That's my ideal day. What's yours?

# WRITER ASSISTANCE PROGRAM

Many companies have Employee Assistance Programs (EAPs). EAPs provide confidential services such as counseling, mental illness assistance, and provider recommendations for childcare, eldercare, and other issues that employees face that inhibit them from doing their jobs to their fullest potential.

EAPs are popular with employers because there is a direct correlation between employee's personal distractions and their work product. As a manager, I can attest to the fact that employees who were having problems at home were not productive. That causes stress for both the employee and the manager.

I'm not praising corporations. They don't provide EAPs out of the goodness of their hearts—trust me on that. The motive seems optimistic on the surface, but corporations are corporations, and that often means capitalistic. And capitalism has a very ugly side. However, I do believe that employees should take advantage of EAPs, assuming that the employer ensures confidentiality. It's free, and it can be effective. I used my company's EAP to seek therapy for the issues I had with my biological father, and it helped me tremendously.

Anyway, this quarter, my 93-year-old grandfather sustained

a life-changing injury that required him to move in with my parents. It was completely unexpected and a difficult adjustment for everyone in my family.

I called my employer's EAP to see what recommendations they had for caregiving providers. They sent me an eldercare kit with some great information that my parents were able to use to give my grandfather better care. All free, and all confidential.

I love the idea of a Writer's Assistance Program. I know that such things do exist; the state of New York used to have a hotline that artists could call for mental health issues and advice regarding their profession. I don't know if that still exists or not.

Writers are all alone with no assistance. Consider that, as a group, we:

- suffer from mental illness and substance abuse at a higher rate than the general population
- have a higher rate of repetitive stress injuries
- struggle to get access to healthcare if we're not employed in a full-time job
- may or may not have spouses and family members who understand our art
- endure money issues because writing doesn't exactly pay the bills for most authors
- have a more difficult tax situation that is truly hard to appreciate until you've experienced it firsthand
- have bills, family obligations, and issues just like everyone else

Yet, what assistance do we receive? None unless we seek it out ourselves.

I envision a Writers Assistance Program that assists writers in their personal lives to help them write to their fullest potential. When writers write more, they make more money.

Such a program might provide:

- programs for substance abuse, addiction, and mental illness, such as a set number of sessions with a certified treatment provider
- resources to help authors reduce repetitive stress injuries, including discounts on equipment
- a referral network of financial advisors, attorneys, and tax accountants who understand authors
- connection to a suicide prevention hotline

This *feels* like something where an existing EAP service provider can tailor their offerings for writers, possibly through a nonprofit organization. It depends on the cost. I believe that authors would gladly pay a slight increase in dues if they knew that the money was going to authors in need, and that the same benefits would be available for them someday. That's how we take care of each other as a community.

# COMMUNITY-SUPPORTED AGRICULTURE...FOR BOOKS?

Community-supported agriculture (CSA) is a way for consumers to buy local, seasonal food directly from a farmer. Typically, you pay a flat fee for a season, and then the farmer delivers food to your home. Or you pick it up at the farm.

There are many CSAs in my state of Iowa. This year, I bought a "salad" package, and every week I had a random green delivered to my doorstep—kale, lettuce, arugula, etc. I ate a lot of salads, but the produce was fantastic. CSAs are a great way to support local agriculture.

What about doing something like this for publishing?

Enter community-sourced publishing (CSPs). Pay a charge, and you'll receive hot new self-published books every week with bonuses. Imagine something like this tailored for a genre, like space opera, mystery, or urban fantasy. The titles could even be exclusive to the CSP for a short time.

I'm sure someone has done this. It's similar to a book club but without discussions.

You can handle the book fulfillment with a service like Book Funnel or Story Origin for ebooks. You can even have a paperback or hardcover option for higher rates, and the paper editions can be fulfilled through automation and drop shipping. You just need a human or two to handle the website, curation and customer service, and author payments.

# WATCH THE MASTER AT WORK

I've been spending time on Twitch lately. It's such a fascinating platform—people will watch a streamer for hours, even if that person isn't doing anything. I watched a livestream of a writer working on their novel draft in Microsoft Word. The camera wasn't even directly pointed at him. He didn't say a word on the stream. He just sat there typing, sighing in frustration, and staring at his computer. That's intriguing to me.

Here's an idea: every day at the same time, go live and share your screen. Tell people what you're working on and then do it. Then answer a few questions here and there. Let people see you outline, research, write, edit, format, publish, and market your book.

Imagine a mega-bestselling author doing this and what aspiring and new authors could learn from simply watching someone's screen. How much time does it take? Not much more than going live and answering a few questions. After all, they're going to be sitting at their computer anyway...

Imagine what amazing instructional lessons an author could build over just a few years. I'm a fan of "documenting" your process and your journey. Let people see how you work and how your writing methods evolve. Sure, you might spoil some of your work ahead of time, but I doubt anyone will care.

This would be captivating even if the author spends time staring at the screen. If it wasn't, then Twitch wouldn't be nearly as popular as it is today. It's no longer a platform for just gamers. I believe someone on YouTube could be successful doing this too.

# AMALGAM FOR SELF-PUBLISHED WRITERS

In the nineties, Marvel and DC Comics organized a collaboration called *Amalgam*, which was a crossover in both universes. The series took place in an alternate universe where Marvel and DC characters were merged.

For example, they took Wolverine and Batman and merged him into a character called Logan Wayne, also known as the Dark Claw. This character is a mixture of both characters; his parents are murdered at a young age, he goes to live with his uncle in Canada, and is the victim of a scientific experiment gone wrong. He swears to use his powers to avenge his parents and fight crime. He has an adamantium skeleton with claws, regenerative healing powers, a utility belt, and is a martial art specialist. And he solves crimes.

The villain of the story was a merge between Sabretooth and the Joker.

Wow!

The *Amalgam* comics were popular among fans because of their creativity. Plus, they were great marketing.

I've often thought about this for my fiction. What if I took two of my fiction series and amalgamated them together? What if I merged both series' heroes, villains, supporting characters, worlds, and plots together?

I imagine that if the right author did this, their fans would lose their minds. But more practically, it would just be a lot of fun. The story would take you in different directions too so it would feel familiar but probably end unexpectedly.

How cool would it be if the series became a discoverability tool? Maybe some readers don't know about one of the series that contributed to the amalgamation, and they rush off and buy it. You'll look like a marketing genius if you're successful.

I love this idea! But you can steal it if you want.

# REVERSING YOUR SERIES

What if you took a series that you already wrote and reversed it?

Turn your hero into a villain but keep the core elements of their personality the same. Transform them from male to female. Change the mood from optimistic to pessimistic. Turn the setting upside-down (if the original story takes place in summer, make the new one in winter, for example) . What would happen?

Do this with an already popular series and it would be a fun experiment. What would readers think? What would happen if the "reversed" series was *more popular* than the existing one?

# KINGDOM HEARTS FOR SELF-PUBLISHED WRITERS

One of my favorite games for the PlayStation 2 was *Kingdom Hearts*. It was a Japanese roleplaying game crossover between the *Final Fantasy* series and the Disney universe.

In the story, the main character, Sora, lives in a peaceful place called The Destiny Islands with his friends, Riku and Kairi. One day, a rift opens, and monsters called Heartless arrive and destroy the islands. Sora is separated from his friends and sucked into the void. He mysteriously lands in a place called Traverse Town, where other people end up as refugees because their worlds were destroyed by the Heartless too. Those people in Traverse Town happen to be characters from the *Final Fantasy* and Disney worlds. Sora meets two characters named Donald and Goofy who are trying to find their king who has gone out to search for a way to defeat the Heartless once and for all—King Mickey Mouse!

Sora travels across the universe to various Disney worlds to protect them from the Heartless. Tarzan, Aladdin, Mulan, the Lion King, and so on. In each world, the Heartless appear and change the timeline of the original Disney film. The game is an epic crossover, possibly one of the most original of all time.

Much like the *Amalgam* idea, wouldn't be interesting if an author did this with their writing?

Imagine a prolific author with many series who creates a new storyline where an original character visits the worlds of the author's most popular series and works with the readers' favorite characters. That's my idea of fun.

An idea like this might not work, but if it does...you'll create raging fans because the series will be a figurative billboard for your entire body of work. It's incredible marketing. Readers will go on to read the worlds represented in the series.

I've been thinking of doing this too, but you can steal it if you want.

# STREAM DECKS FOR PUBLISHING

I recently purchased an Elgato Stream Deck for use in my livestreams. The deck sits on my desk and has 15 gel buttons that I can press that activate features on my computer.

In video conferencing programs, I can use Stream Deck buttons to go live and end broadcasts, change scenes, mute and unmute, turn my webcam on and off, bring in guests, share my screen, and more.

In Microsoft PowerPoint, I can control the flow of my slides.

In Google Chrome, I can map bookmark websites to a button. I can even launch multiple websites with a button.

Even better, I can use hotkeys and map those to buttons on my Stream Deck so I can use it with any program as long as it supports hotkeys. This got me thinking about how a Stream Deck can be a helpful productivity tool:

- While researching my novel, I can bring up websites such as Wikipedia, dictionaries, YouTube, or more with the click of a button. This saves time.
- While writing and editing my novel, I can map simple functions like copy, paste, cut, split-screen,

word count revealer, and export into a single key. Again, this saves me a few fractions of a second because I don't have to type the hotkeys. I just push a button.

- When I'm ready to publish, I can launch all of my retailer dashboards with the push of a button. I can also use this to review my sales.
- If I want to see how a certain book is performing, I can launch the book's sales page at all retailers.
- When I'm doing Microsoft Excel work, I can map macros to a button. This will save clicks.

Is the Stream Deck the ultimate productivity tool? No. It has limitations, but it can save time. I've never liked hotkeys on the Mac; I find them too difficult to execute without having to look down at the keyboard. It's easier to press a button. It's not ergonomic, but I don't use the Stream Deck often enough for it to be an issue.

# THE OPPOSITE YEAR CHALLENGE

What if, every day, for a year, you did the exact opposite of your publishing instincts?

When your critical voice says, "Don't write your novel without outlining," write without an outline.

When you tell yourself you can't do something, do it anyway.

When a marketing idea sounds repulsive to you, try it.

What would happen? What would you learn?

I believe our instinct exists to protect us and guide us in the right direction. I also believe that sometimes our instincts can be wrong. In my experience, I find that my instinct is right around 90 percent of the time when it comes to major decisions. What about that other 10 percent?

I bet many of your choices wouldn't work out, but what if one amazing thing happened? What if it changed your career? What if it brought in readers and money in ways you never dreamed? That's why this challenge intrigues me, and I believe it would be great for introverted writers who lack confidence in their publishing endeavors. Nothing gives you confidence better than doing something that turns out well unexpectedly.

# MEDITATION MP3S FOR WRITERS

Last year on my YouTube channel, someone recommended that I do meditation MP3s. I always liked the idea but never got around to it. It's not high on my priority list, so I'm releasing it to the public.

Here's the idea: do a series of MP3s that help writers build their confidence and focus on their stories. In five minutes, state affirmations and give them prompts to think about their story.

"Imagine that you have published your book and that you are successful. Your family is proud, readers are sending you fan-mail every day, your bank account is overflowing with money. All the negative emotions you feel right now will be a distant memory, and you won't remember them."

"Visualize your self-doubt as a wispy ball of energy. Inhale, and when you exhale, imagine that energy dissipating like salt evaporating in water."

"Think back to the last section in your novel. What did you write? As you think about it, let your mind drift..."

Sync your voice to calming, royalty-free music and create MP3s for different tasks: one set for writing, another for editing, etc. Writers can use them before they start writing for the day or whenever they get stuck.

# ROADMAPS

Every app has a "roadmap" these days. Over the past few years, developers have created pages on their websites that show what features they are working on. Some developers even allow users to vote on what they want next, and the developers prioritize accordingly. I've always thought roadmaps were a good transparency tool and a great community builder.

What if an author created a roadmap tool? Create a page on your site with works-in-progress and the next books you plan on writing. Let readers vote on which ones they want to see and prioritize your workload accordingly.

I like the idea because it lets readers participate in your vision for your portfolio, but you're always in control. After all, they're voting on books *you already want to write.* That's the magic behind a tool like this. If you let readers tell you to write books you're not passionate about, then this idea will fail.

## COFFEE AND TEA BRANDS FOR AUTHORS

I've always wondered why influencers in the writing space haven't been more aligned with coffee and tea brands. Coffee is the patron saint of writers.

If you're a popular influencer, why not:

- Cultivate a sponsorship with a coffee or tea brand.
- Approach a coffee or tea brand about partnering on a line of blends geared toward writers and creatives.
- Collaborate with a coffee or tea label to create your brand of writing coffee or tea.

There's some risk, of course. Sponsors come with demands. Any time you put your name on a product, you can be sued for products liability if someone gets sick (so you'll need insurance). There's also the problem of trademarks. But liability and legal concerns aside, it's a great idea and one that would make an influencer a lot of money. I've only seen one influencer on YouTube do this, so there's an opportunity here.

# BRING ESSAYS BACK

I've always loved essays. Not high school essays (boo), but traditional essays in the spirit of writers like G.K. Chesterton and James Baldwin.

An essay is an author's opinion about a certain topic, written in a highly stylized form. One of my favorite examples of an essay is *In Praise of Shadows* by Junichiro Tanizaki, which is a celebration of the Japanese aesthetic.

I like essays because they memorialize the times in which they're written. They're also an amazing way to broaden your perspective on an issue. Imagine how much better our world would be today if people wrote well-reasoned essays in favor of their opinions and refuting others'. That's a far better world than the one we currently inhabit, where people just yell at each other on news shows and social media. Writers like James Baldwin changed the world by channeling thoughts that many black people had about racism but couldn't articulate. Throughout history, there have been countless other men and women who changed the world with well-reasoned arguments on the page.

Essays are still alive, but they have fallen out of favor in shaping the culture. No one talks about essays around the watercooler at work. That said, you could argue that certain YouTube videos are a continuation of the modern essay in video form. Casey Neistat is a good example of this kind of YouTuber. He published a video about how irritated he was with a New York City bike lane on the Williamsburg Bridge, and the video went so viral that the city did something about it.

And, of course, writers everywhere are familiar with the classic essay collections *On Writing* by Stephen King and *Bird by Bird* by Anne Lamott. Essays are alive and well, but I wish that they were more popular, that's all.

I've had an idea for a long time to write a collection of formal essays on self-publishing. Maybe I'll do it someday, but in the meantime, I believe essays will come back in the future.

# IDEAS THAT HAVE WORKED WELL FOR ME IN THE LAST DECADE

I thought it would be a good idea to cap this book with an analysis of ideas that have worked well for me over the past eight years as a self-published writer. Also, it's my attempt to show that I come up with crazy ideas all the time, and some of them work. Maybe these ideas will work for you, or maybe they won't, but you never know unless you try.

**Hermetic behavior.** I don't do very much when I'm not working other than write or think about writing. I've given up almost every hobby except for listening to jazz and video game music. And I do watch a lot of YouTube. But other than that, writing is my sole focus. I've paid a price for it in other areas of my life—namely I don't have much of a social life—but the price was worth it.

**Pilot series**. Once upon a time, I had two ideas for series and couldn't decide which one to write, so I asked my readers to help me. I wrote two series "pilots" with one chapter each and shared them with my readers. Readers voted on the one they liked best, and I turned that into a series. The winning series was *Android X*, which was my first fiction success as an author.

**Crazy series.** I wrote a series about the wackiest idea I could think of: a gang of anthropomorphic vegetable terrorists fighting to take down a civilization of processed foods. This was my *Moderation Online* series, and it was a spectacular flop. However, the readers who like it really like it. The concept is always good for a giggle, and people regularly pick it up because it sounds so ridiculous that they have to see it for themselves.

**Treat your work like an ant colony**. In 2015, I had an infestation of carpenter ants in my home. Strangely, the experience taught me to think of my books like ants. Every book you write is an ant that you send out into the world. Some ants never return; others return with money and opportunities. Every piece of media you create is an ant too, such as blogs, videos, and podcasts. But you don't start seeing ants return until you send a *lot* of them into the world. Being prolific is a smart long-term strategy.

**Treat your portfolio like a portfolio**. Every book you write becomes part of a portfolio of assets. Treat your book like you'd treat real estate. Every few years, you need to update your covers, book descriptions, and metadata. Some assets are worth more than others, but they all contribute to the overall value of your portfolio.

**Be first.** In 2015, I published a book called *Indie Poet Rock Star: The Poet's Guide to Ebooks, Marketing, and the Self-Publishing Revolution*. It was a courageous book because I predicted that self-publishing would transform the poetry world. Around this time, poets and poetry readers were resistant to ebooks and self-publishing. Many of the predictions in the book came true. I didn't care if anyone read the book, but it turns out someone important did, and it led to amazing opportunities to work for The Alliance of Independent Authors, which led to getting introduced to Writer's Digest, which led to getting face-time with Apple Books, which led to...you get the idea.

**Be last**. Sometimes, you don't want to adopt something right away. Let other people figure it out.

**Nonprofit outreach.** I devote time each month to The Alliance of Independent Authors, and it has led to amazing opportunities. But most importantly, I love giving back to the author community by contributing to a cause I believe in.

**Unified branding.** In 2016, I decided to go with a similar look all of my book covers. I created a design for fiction, nonfiction, and poetry. That went a long way to improving the overall look of my portfolio.

**Be willing to talk to a wall.** If you look at my multi-media efforts (YouTube, podcasting, blogging, etc.), I started with nothing. My very first podcast was a 10-minute show where I talked about what was on my mind while I drove to the gym every week. For later podcasts, I talked to a wall and published that conversation. Slowly, people started paying attention. That never would have happened if I didn't dare to put stuff into the universe with no expectation of return.

**"The Writer's Journey" Podcast.** I did a podcast for two years, and it was immensely popular. The only content was about me and the issues I was dealing with. I learned that people love to see behind the scenes how others work and what they're thinking.

**"Writing Tip of the Day" Podcast.** For two years, I released a podcast that shared a crisp writing tip in five minutes or less. At the time of this writing, it was my most popular show of all time.

**Set a clear strategy.** I'm not saying that people have to follow my strategy, but taking the time to craft a clear strategy helped me win big in 2020 during the pandemic. I learned that when you take the time to be clear about what you want out of your author career and work toward your goals, the universe will reward you for it.

**Writing in public.** I learned this from Dean Wesley Smith. He publishes a daily journal blog post on his website every day and tells people what he did to move his writing business forward every day. I did the same thing, and it worked very well for me.

**Float test ideas.** I've had ideas that I felt strongly about but my audience didn't like. Whenever I have an idea, I "float it" to my audience on my blog to see what the response is. If it doesn't connect, I'll float it again. If it fails twice, then it's not something they want. I did this with my editing engine and it saved me time and effort—I thought maybe people would be interested in building something similar for themselves, but they weren't.

**Blue ocean strategy.** I've built a name for myself in the writing space by tackling ideas that others won't touch. My *Writing Craft Playbook* is a series of drawings that show writers how mega bestsellers write their fiction. I was inspired by watching a football game one day. I'm willing to go places no one else will go, and I've been rewarded for it.

**Collaboration.** I wrote a series (*Modern Necromancy*) with my friend Justin Sloan. It was successful and it grew both our audiences. I would collaborate with someone again if it was the right project.

**Beast Mode.** I made a public goal of writing as many books as possible in 90 days, and my community loved it. I called it my "Beast Mode Challenge." It increased my portfolio count and brought great engagement to my platform.

**Synergizing my personal, professional, and writing life.** I see my insurance work, writing, and personal life as harmonizing forces. My goal is to ensure that they're playing a great song. Many people hate their jobs and don't want to think about them outside of work. I happened to enjoy my work and used many benefits that my employers offered to further my writing business. My employer paid for law school, therapy, and so on. I applied lessons I learned at work to my writing, especially with data and analytics. I kept getting promoted, which afforded me better opportunities and more time to write.

**Writing on the go.** Pre-pandemic, I owed 40 percent of my word counts to writing on my phone. At first, I didn't like the idea of writing on my phone, but it was so successful for me that I relearned how to write novels. I consider it one of my superpowers along with dictation.

**Use speaking engagements to pay for technology.** Every time I land a paid speaking engagement, I use that money to reinvest in my technology. I believe this is a competitive advantage. It allows me to upgrade my online presence cost-free.

**Capture ideas like Pokémon.** I'm religious about writing ideas down. I have notebooks full of ideas, and that ensures that I never run out of ideas.

**Practice idea sex (also known as idea calculus).** I learned this from Claudia Azula Altucher in her book *Become an Idea Machine*. I come up with new ideas every day and mix ideas in unusual ways.

**Test runs.** When I take on projects, I do it because of what I will learn. I often "test" a project on a small scale. When I created my first course, *Write to Market*, I did it as an experiment. I broke a lot of rules and figured out how to create a course. The next year, when I created my course, *Writing in Hard Times*, I did it in a third of the time, at a much higher production level. That taught me how to make a seriously good premium course. To date, I have made very little from my courses, but I was willing to invest that time and energy to learn how to create them.

**Be willing to go down rabbit holes.** I like to explore ideas just to see what happens. Most people are far more pragmatic than I am; they'll decline anything that doesn't suit their immediate needs. I'll dissect an idea for the idea's sake even if I know it possibly won't go anywhere. I do it because of the knowledge. Knowledge is power. When you accumulate knowledge, you can use it to inform your strategy and aid your tactical execution. For example, I saw someone use a Microsoft Excel macro once, and a voice in the back of my head told me to explore it. Dozens of hours later, I had created an automated sales report process. I had no idea where the journey would take me, but I'm glad I took it. Several months later, I successfully automated parts of my editing. All because I was willing to explore an idea that most people would have written off because they either weren't interested or willing to learn how it could help them.

To give you another example, I provided a consultation to a Silicon Valley company for a tool that can help authors manage their intellectual property. The project lasted several months. We hit a dead-end, but the knowledge I learned was extremely valuable because I know how to build a tool like this in the future. The project was a masterclass in working with developers and shrewd businesspeople.

To be fair, most of my expeditions don't end this way, but I'm willing to go on 100 expeditions if 20 of them produce treasure. Each treasure is a competitive advantage in the long term.

Those are just a few of the ideas that helped me get where I am today. Feel free to steal them for yourself. If you do, I hope they work for you as well, if not better than they did for me.

## CONTENT CREATED WHILE WRITING THIS BOOK

**Author Level Up YouTube Channel - Highlights**

Watch at youtube.com/authorlevelup.

New Studio Setup. See Michael's new YouTube setup in action.

Scrivener 3 for Windows: First Impressions. Now that Scrivener 3 is available for Windows, hear Michael's thoughts.

How I Deal with Overwhelm as a Writer. Hear Michael's thoughts on how he approaches stressful times.

**Interviews & Appearances**

"The Curiously Effective Power of Drifting." Article in the print version of Writer's Digest, May/June 2021. Look for it wherever you get your magazines.

## READ THE NEXT VOLUME

Michael's writer journey continues in the next volume of this series!

Grab your copy at www.authorlevelup.com/confidential.

# MEET M.L. RONN

Science fiction and fantasy on the wild side!

M.L. Ronn (Michael La Ronn) is the author of many science fiction and fantasy novels including *The Good Necromancer, Android X,* and *The Last Dragon Lord* series.

In 2012, a life-threatening illness made him realize that storytelling was his #1 passion. He's devoted his life to writing ever since, making up whatever story makes him fall out of his chair laughing the hardest. Every day.

*Learn more about Michael*
www.authorlevelup.com (for writers)
www.michaellaronn.com (fiction)

# MORE BOOKS BY M.L. RONN

**Books for Writers:**

www.authorlevelup.com/books

**Fiction:**
www.michaellaronn.com/books